Gas Station Collectibles

Mitch Stenzler and Rick Pease

Schiffer Publishing Ltd

77 Lower Valley Road, Atglen, PA 19310

Exceptionally rare chimney top globe for Excelsior Motor Gasoline, Mills Oil Co. The chimney top globes are probably the most rare and most desirable of all globes dating back to 1912.

Dedication

This book is dedicated to the memory of Mitch Stenzler who loved life and loved collecting. He had hoped to share some of his knowledge and enthusiasm with other collectors. It is also dedicated to Rick Pease who made Mitch's dream of a book come true.

We want to thank the following people who contributed so much through their knowledge and/or sharing their collections with us:

Ken Boone, George Maddox, Chuck Pergl and Lee Pergl.

Published by Schiffer Publishing, Ltd.
77 Lower Valley Road
Atglen, PA 19310
Please write for a free catalog.
This book may be purchased from the publisher.
Please include $2.95 postage.
Try your bookstore first.

We are interested in hearing from authors
with book ideas on related subjects.

Copyright © 1993 by Sonya Stenzler and Rick Pease
Library of Congress Catalog Number: 93-83049.

Printed in China
ISBN: 0-88740-496-0

CONTENTS

INTRODUCTION

I have long loved antique automobiles and the old service stations that catered to their every need. Growing up in the 30s, I had experience of gas stations that were concerned with far more than gasoline. I remember sitting in the back seat of my dad's big car when he pulled into his favorite "service station." Five attendants rushed to the car. One would have the hood up checking the fluids, while another was on one knee checking the tire pressure. I would be watching the guy with the big chamois washing the windshield. While all this was going on, I could count the gallons going into the tank by counting the dings the pump made, one ding for every gallon.

The original attendant by now had asked my dad to step out of the car and, with a small wisk broom taken from his back pocket, he swept out the floor on the driver's side. Oh yes, all the attendants wore neat uniforms complete with a cap and a leather bow tie.

The "main guy" in my little boy eyes made change and sometimes came back to the car with a wonderful surprise, a game or a key chain or something that was super. If we were going to take a short trip, we would pick up a few maps, free of course. The thirties were truly the golden age of service station collectibles.

Giveaways, however, started back when the first automobiles took to the American road. "Gasolene," as it was originally spelled, was first dispensed at the general store, but that changed rather quickly. As competition grew so did marketing ideas. In those early days of the service station one couldn't miss those ten foot tall metal giants that stood majestically in front so all the cars could pull within easy range. These pumps were crowned with a beautiful globe.

The earliest globes merely said "Gasolene." A little later they began to advertise "Filtered Gasoline." Before long brand names began to appear, and with them came the glass globe that was illuminated from within.

Globe collectors will note that there are some basic differences in globes. There are one-piece glass globes, metal band globes with glass faces, front and back, and three-piece glass globes with a glass body and glass faces, front and back. As the 30s began, the style of globes with a plastic body holding glass faces emerged and became most common. Values on globes vary, but one could safely say that the earlier one-piece globes with multi-colors and detailed graphics are certainly a valuable asset in a globe collection. The same formula follows to the other types of globes, detail and color being an important strong point. As with all collectibles, condition, rarity, supply and demand dictate globe prices.

The prices of other service station collectibles can vary, depending on the uniqueness of the item as well as its condition. When that unique item, the thing that hasn't shown up before, is discovered, the collector feels a "rush" that can't be beat. This is especially true when the item is in excellent condition.

License plate attachments are getting nearly impossible to find in decent shape. These items were used from the very early days of automobiles to the late 50s, when the design of the cars left no place for these great little goodies. I call them the early day bumper stickers, and the more unusual they are the better it is for the collector.

Ashtrays have also been a good collectible. The earliest that I know of was an all glass ashtray made by the Pennsylvania Rubber Co., called the Non Skid Vacuum Cup. Ashtrays were mostly made with a glass insert in a rubber tire. The most collectible are those with a logo or slogan embossed into the glass. Mobil made a few with a bronze Pegasus standing on top of the ashtray. These have all but disappeared from the market.

Nobody really knows how many service station collectibles there are. It seems like all the really interesting ones are already in the hands of collectors, but in fact there are still some waiting to be found. In the spring of 1989 I was able to obtain one of my best pieces, a penknife in the shape of a 1930s gas pump with an Esso globe. There are still wonderful pieces to collect. Road maps, match holders, mechanical pencils, playing cards, key chains, watch fobs; the list goes on and on.

Among the best items from the 40s to the early 60s were the little oil can banks. Most were round like cans but some were in the shape of gas pumps, dinosaurs, clam shells, or glass bricks. Some were in the shape of little fat men (six different kinds are known). Texaco made banks in the shape of intricate gas pumps, with a globe and a hose and nozzle. A bell would ring when a coin was deposited.

Another area of service station collecting includes the displays and other items from inside and outside the station. Schrader tire gauge displays are very popular and getting very scarce in good condition. Porcelain signs as well as lighter weight pressed tin signs are also very popular. And, believe it or not, some people even collect the entire station. Yes, I mean they pick it up and move it or dismantle it and rebuild it in their back yard or wherever.

Collectors should obtain as many different pieces for their collection as their wallet can afford. Even if the item you find isn't the best, it will hold a place until a better one comes along. Just remember the difference between a collector and an accumulator. To be a collector one needs to know the when and where of an item, and fit it into his or her collection with some type of organization.

Mitch Stenzler

GLOBES

One-piece Globes

These desirable globes are one-piece milk glass. They vary in advertising from simple to elaborative. Like all globes, these provided a way to advertise the different trademarks. They were used by small and large oil companies alike. They date from 1912 to the 1940s.

One-piece glass globe for Seiberling All-Treads tires. Very rare.

Delco Gasoline glass globe. One-piece, with Independent Oil trademark.

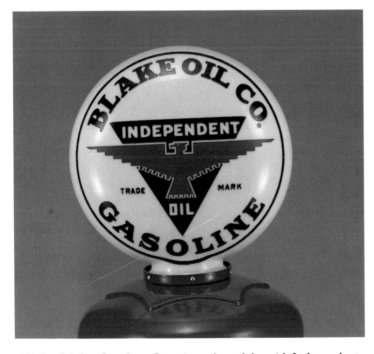

Blake Oil Co. Gasoline. One-piece glass globe with Independent Oil trade mark.

This was used to advertise service at dealership (etched).

Galtex, advertising their gasoline and motor oils.

Tryon Pep-Po Motor Fuel one-piece globe.

Gulf one-piece globe.

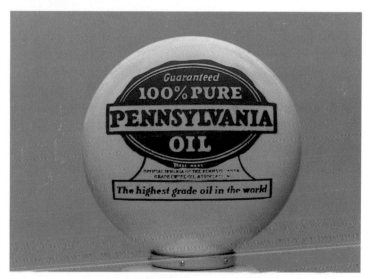

Pennsylvania Oil one-piece globe.

A pre-Texaco etched one-piece Indian Gas globe, featuring the Havoline name.

Sinclair Aircraft one-piece globe.

Shellmex shell-shaped globe.

One-piece Super-Shell globe.

Round generic globe marked "Visible Gasoline."

Rare Shell globe.

One-piece globe for Texaco Ethyl gasoline.

Metal-band Globes

The metal band globes are from the same era as the one piece globes. They are probably the most colorful and detailed of all globes. Some of the independent oil companies offered the most picturesque of the metal band globes. They advertised everything from kerosene to tires. They date from 1914 to 1922.

Blue Streak Gasoline globe with metal band.

This metal band globe for Atlantic Rayolight Kerosene is not easy to find.

Elim-A-Nox Gasoline from Oil Creek used this metal banded globe with nice graphics.

Metal band globe for Betholine Motor Fuel.

Metal band globe for Crystal Flash Gas.

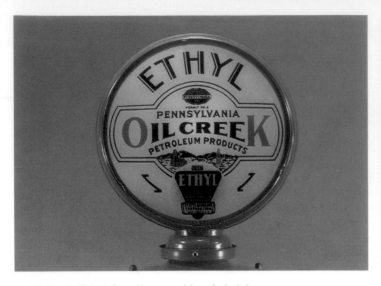

Oil Creek Ethyl Gasoline metal banded globe.

Generic metal banded globe.

Justfine Gasoline from Oil Creek, metal banded globe.

This is an extremely collectible metal banded globe for Gilmore gasoline.

Metal banded globe for Eldred High Test.

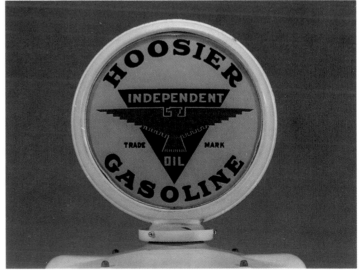

Hoosier Gasoline globe with Independent Oil trade mark.

Hart Gasoline Motor Oils banded globe.

A very rare banded glove for Indian Oil Products Co.'s Aerolene gasoline.

This Illinois Oil Co. banded globe features a torpedo.

A very colorful banded globe with outstanding art work for Independent Gasoline.

A rare metal banded globe for Socony Burning Oil, pre-dating Mobil.

A rare metal banded glove for Aero Mobilgas.

The great art on this globe is for Gargoyle Mobiloil. Metro Gas Station was Mobil.

Penco Gasoline banded globe.

The graphics of this Me-tee-or Gasoline banded globe, give it the feeling of power and movement.

Rare Purgo Radiator Service metal banded globe.

Nicolene Gasolene banded globe with the trade mark of the National Independent Oil Company in the center.

The stylized eagle is nicely executed on this Penn-O-Lene banded globe.

Rare Nicolene Kerosene banded globe.

Richfield metal banded globe with an interesting use of colors.

A very unusual banded globe for Nonpareil Silent Gasoline.

Sears Premium gasoline. Upstate New York.

Metal banded globe with Richfield Gasoline logo.

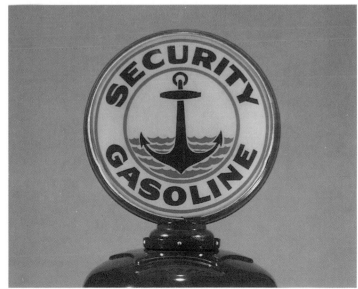

Metal banded Security Gasoline globe.

Sunoco Dynafuel banded globe.

Very rare banded globe with milk glass Texaco insert.

Socony banded globe with an unusual attachment.

Colorful banded globe for Tiwoser High Test Gasoline. Nice graphics.

Metal banded Skyhawk Gasoline globe with nice graphics.

Tydol Flying A gasoline banded globe. Used in the transition from Tydol to Flying A.

Atlantic White Flash gasoline banded globe with attachment.

Wings gill body globe with nice graphics.

Metal banded globe for Pure Webaco Gas.

Gill Body Globes

The gill body globes are very colorful, with some having a ripple rather than a smooth body. The Wings Ethyl is a good example of the ripple body. The ripple body is the most desirable of the gill body globes because of the bright colors and the limited number which were produced. They date from 1930 to the 1940s.

Ripple gill body globe for Kan O Tex gasoline.

A gill body globe for Guyler Brand Gasoline. The metal band holds the lens to the body.

Orange ripple gill body globe for Texan gasoline.

Gill body globe for Hall Bros. Kerosene.

CrownZol gasoline gill body globe.

A very collectible, nicely illustrated gill body globe for Kan O Tex aviation fuel.

Three-piece Glass Globes

The three-piece, milk glass gasoline globes were the most common and widely used globes in the late 1940s. These globes were used for a longer period of time than the other types. This was probably due to the globe's durability as well as its being a cost effective advertising tool. They dated from the 1920s to the 1940s.

Super A Gasoline three-piece globe.

Tydol Ethyl aviation fuel is advertised on this gill body globe.

Sterling Gasoline three-piece glass globe with advertisement for Quaker State oil.

Stephen gasoline three-piece globe.

Three-piece glass globe for Senzo Seneca Chief Benzol Motor Fuel.

Frontier Double Refined gasoline globe.

Staroline Gasoline three-piece glass globe.

Golden 102 Premium Gasoline globe, three-piece.

G.L.F. Quality gasoline globe.

I.Q.S. Regular three-piece glass globe.

One of the nicest picture globes is this Iroquois Chief three-piece glass globe.

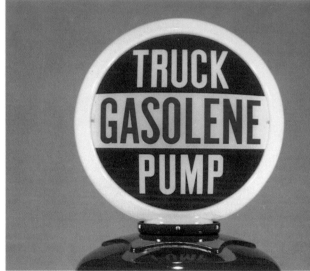

Unique globe advertisement for trucks. Three-piece glass.

I.Q.S., Independent Quality Service three-piece glass globe.

One of the best picture globe, this one for American Ga features good use of colors and strong graphics. Three glass.

Emolene Blue Gasoline. Three-piece glass globe.

Save-More Ethyl System globe with nice graphics.

Sinclair Gasoline. Three-piece glass globe.

Sohio (Standard of Ohio) Aviation fuel globe. Three-piece glass.

Very colorful Shamrock globe. Three-piece glass.

Dixie Oils and Gasoline three-piece glass globe in a very unusual shape.

DX Ethyl three-piece glass globe.

Clymer Blue First Grade Anti-Knock globe. Three-piece glass.

Diamond Power "G" globe.

Blu-Flame globe for Zepher Kerosene with nice graphics. Three-piece glass.

Bolivar Gasoline globe from Allegheny Refiners. Bolivar, New York.

Wolf's Head three-piece glass globe.

Wides "Gas for Less" glass globe. Three-piece.

Wadhams Metro glass globe.

Three-piece Vance Premium Ethyl gasoline globe.

Marine gasoline three-piece glass gasoline globe.

Plastic Body Globes

The plastic gasoline globes were introduced in the 1940s as trends began to change. In some instances, these globes were used through the 1960s by small independents. The body was in two parts which was made of plastic and faces were all glass-body plastic!

Keystone plastic globe with attachment.

Plastic globe for Keystone regular gasoline.

Hudson Regular gasoline plastic globe with some of the better art work.

Indiana Premium gasoline plastic globe.

Hico High Compression aviation fuel plastic.

Indiana Ethyl gasoline plastic globe.

Red Feather gasoline plastic globe.

Plastic globe for Phillips Unique gasoline.

Rock Island Rockilene gasoline. Plastic globe.

Rare plastic Sinclair SuperFlame Kerosene globe.

Rock Island gasoline plastic globe.

Savings Golden Premium globe.

Oval Clipper plastic globe.

A plastic eyecatcher for Col-Tex.

Champlin Gasoline's red, white and blue plastic globe was made in four pieces.

Lady Liberty hails all drivers from this plastic globe.

A "honey" of a globe for Beeline Gasoline, in plastic.

This Wood River globe in plastic.

A plastic globe for Valvoline's Go-Mix outboard fuel.

Wides Oil Co.' globe is plastic.

This very unusual picture globe for Tankar in plastic.

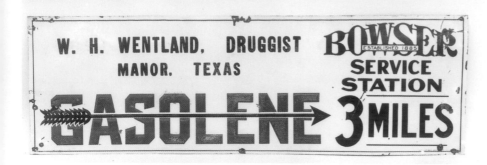

A very early (circa 1905) tin sign for Bowser Gasolene, one of the early manufacturers. 11½″ x 35½″.

A checkerboard flag from Mobil service stations in the 1960s, 21½″ x 24.

A Rocolene oil dispenser sign from the 1940s, 7″ diam.

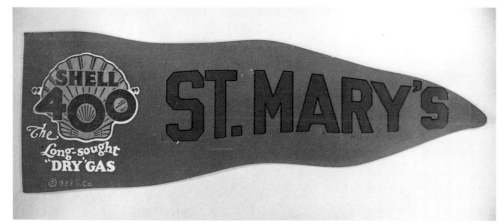

A pennant for St. Mary's, with the crest of their sponsor, Shell. 3¾″ x 11¼″, 1928.

A Mobil oil dispenser sign from the 1920s, 8″ diam.

An Oil Creek Service Station window poster, circa 1925.

Another 1950s Texaco poster for the holidays, 14" x 24.

Seasons Greetings from this Texaco poster from the 1950s, 13" x 17".

Ed Wynn clowns around on this 1934 poster, advertising the comedian's Texaco-sponsored radio show on NBC.

A Texaco magazine advertisement from the late 1920s.

This Shell ad from the 1940s wants to "strike a blow for safety and economy" by criticizing careless drivers and pedestrians.

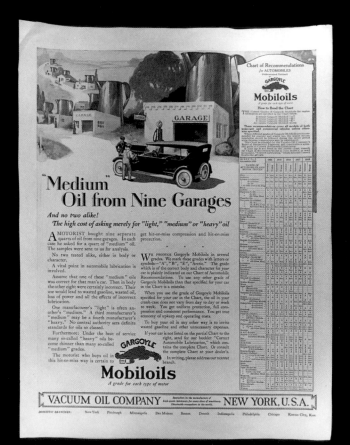

Mobil advertises its line of oils in this 1921 ad.

A 1940 Wayne Pump ad from *Life* magazine.

A winter ad from Texaco, 1931.

A 1905 advertisement from *The American Magazine*.

This *Life* magazine ad from the mid-1930s informs motorists that Socony-Vacuum stations will have a new look.

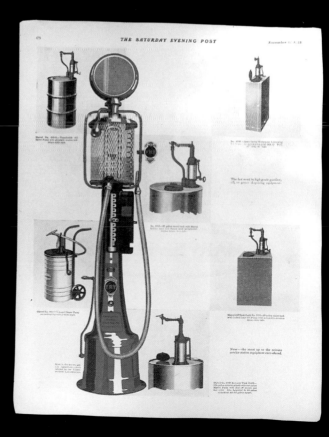

Fry Pump's more technical, less exciting ad from a later 1925 *Saturday Evening Post*.

Fry Pump's Jimmy the Courtesy Man and his "captivating smile" beam out from the pages of this 1926 *Saturday Evening Post*.

A 1926 Independent Oil ad from the *Saturday Evening Post*.

"Smiling he meets you!uu! Smiling he greets you! Smiling he serves you!you!" The Fry Courtesy man never quits.

Wayne's "Honest Measure" pumps advertised in the *Saturday Evening Post* in the mid-1920s.

Mobiloil suggests that drivers keep an emergency supply of motor oil on hand in this ad, circa 1930.

A vividly illustrated ad from Texaco, 1932.

Mobil suggests its "E" oil for all Fords, and provides a chart of recommendations for other makes and years in this ad from the early 1920s.

A watercolor graphic decorates this Texaco gasoline ad from the winter of 1930.

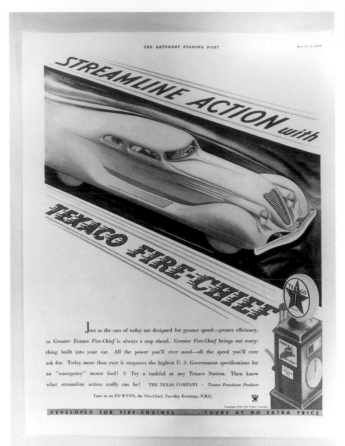

A salesman's sample of the reflective Texaco sign, 15″ long and 9″ high.

Above:
Texaco promises "Streamline Action" and excitement from their 1934 Fire-Chief ad.

Right:
Windshield decals of the Texaco bears (entire sheet 4¼″ x 6″).

Below:
These 1928 Texaco Golden Motor Oil users are winners both on the tennis courts and on the road.

A travelling salesman's model of a Bowser oil or kerosene dispenser, only 3 in. x 4⅛ in.

LICENSE PLATE ORNAMENTS

"Woody's Service," a Texaco station in Illinois, released this 5⅝" x 4¾" license plate ornament.

Phillips 66's trademark orange logo urged drivers to stay safe on this license plate attachment, 5⅜" x 6".

Flying "A" Gasoline boasted of "Giant Power" on this 4⅛" x 6½" license plate ornament.

This diamond-shaped license plate ornament, 4⅛" x 5½", advertises D-X gasoline.

One Ford-Mercury agency's advertisement ornament, 3" x 10".

Pure Oil's banner recommends safe driving to motorists on this 4⅛″ x 7⅝″ license plate ornament.

Dixie gasoline will give your car the "Power to Pass," says this 5½″ x 6¼″ license plate attachment.

The Chicago Motor Club's plate ornament, 6¼″x 11″.

Conoco's "Made in the U.S.A." license plate ornament, 4⅛″ x 2⅝″.

Crown Gasoline urges drivers to be safe, on this 3¾″ x 4¾″ tag.

Hometown pride shows on this decorative license plate attachment from Springdale, Arkansas, 4″ x 12″ in cast aluminum.

In pressed tin, a plate attachment from Fort Worth. 2⅝″ x 10⅜″.

Bausch and Lomb's tag tells drivers to make sure their eyes are in good shape.

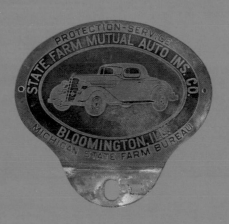

A potentially controversial suggestion of neutrality, 6″ x 4″.

State Farm Insurance's oval tag, 4″ x 4⅛″.

Kansas' Farm Bureau Mutual Insurance put out a tag ornament to brighten the stormiest of drives, 3″ x 4″.

Pure Oil says "Drive Safely," 6″ x 7⅝″.

Hip reflector tag, "Get in the Groove," 4¾" x 5½".

This leering cat tag attachment wiggles its orange eyes when its tongue is pulled. 5" x 4¼".

"How am I Doin?" simpers the next reflector, 4¾" x 5½".

Lady Liberty and her favorite sentiment on this 5⅞" x 5⅞" 1949 tag ornament.

A General Auto Service tag, with phone number, 4¾" x 3⅜".

This reflector (same size) sheds a little light on the subject: "Yeh, man!"

The Liberty Bell, on a plate attachment sponsored by the Young Democratic Clubs of America from 1936. 6″ x 6¼″.

Iowa's State Insurance tag reminds drivers to keep their minds from wandering. 5½″ x 4½″.

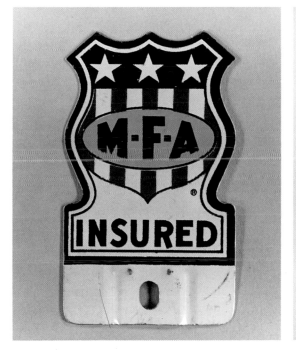

An ornament for drivers insured by MFA, 4¾″ x 2¾″.

A tag attachment marking cars used by Standard Oil's research team. 5¼″ x 9⅛″.

Ford shortens the long arm of the law for this 4″ x 7¾″ tag.

A tag from Metal Auto Parts Co., 6⅞″ x 5⅜″.

A textured tag attachment for Globe gasoline, 5¾″ x 3¾″.

A black cat advertisement for Prest-o-lite batteries, 6⅞″ x 5⅜″.

A Willkie shield ornament, 5″ x 3⅛″.

Willkie and McNary are the Republican team endorsed by this tag,
6″ x 4″.

A campaign tag put out by a Local 809 union in support of Willkie.

A strikingly illustrated ornament from Lions International, 6⅞″ x 4⅛″.

"Drink Zesto: Drive Safely," warns this black and yellow attachment, 5¾″ x 6¼″.

A bell waits to ring out for "Good Roads" on this two-toned metallic tag from the Automobile Club of Southern California, 5 x 3¾″.

A similar tag, painted. 4⅞″ x 3¾″.

A couple of toddlers fall in love over this tag ornament advertising Squeeze beverages, 6″ x 6¼″.

"V" is for Victory, tag ornament, 6″ x 4″.

A very round mechanic from Veedol Gasoline chases customers, 6¾″ x 4½″.

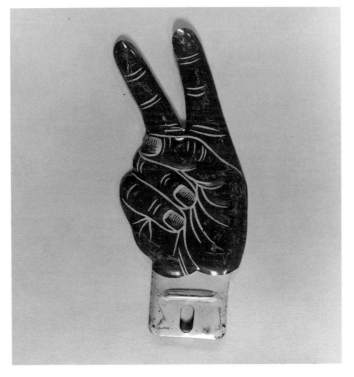

"V" is for Victory again, in not so many words. The hand is 6″ x 2½″.

A smart red and black tag ornament from The Hartford Steam Boiler Inspection and Insurance Co., 5¼″ x 5⅛″.

A reflector tag attachment sold to raise money for the American Olympic Fund in 1940. 4⅝″ x 3⅜″.

The Silvertown Safety League teams up with Goodrich Tires to produce this tag attachment, 5⅜" x 2¼".

A tag attachment for honor members of the Louisville, Kentucky AAA, 5¼" x 3½".

M.J. Wilson Auto Co., a Ford dealership, advertises on this 7½" x 5½" tag.

Marathon's runner logo on a red reflector ornament, 5" x 3¾".

Farm Bureau Insurance advertises their cooperative with this tag attachment, 5¼" x 3½".

Brilliant Bronze's safety reflector tag, 4¼" x 3⅜".

The Railway Express Agency advertises on car license plates! Trains are fast and safe, promises this one, 5⅜" x 6¼".

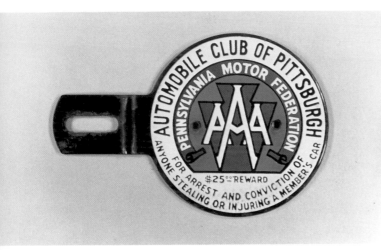

Pittsburgh's Triple-A members sport this foreboding tag—which offers a $25 reward for the "arrest and conviction" of anyone stealing or injuring the car. 3½" x 5¼".

"Take it Easy," urges Easy Washing Machine Corp. on this 1939 tag, 4⅝" x 4¾".

State Farm Insurance's 4¼" x 4¼" tag attachment.

An American flag ripples in the exhaust on this 5½" x 6½" tag.

Pure Oil Co.'s Pledge, on a 5¾" x 9½" tag.

For safety, "Leave it to Landon". 4¾" x 3⅞".

Farmers Automobile Insurance's fan-shaped tag ornament, 3½" x 4½" in bronze-colored metal.

Uncle Sam and a pint-sized eagle endorse Alf Landon on this 5" x 5½" ornament.

Another campaign plate featuring the G.O.P. elephant; 4⅜" x 11¾".

The Farmers Automobile Insurance tag, painted in primary colors. 3½" x 4½"

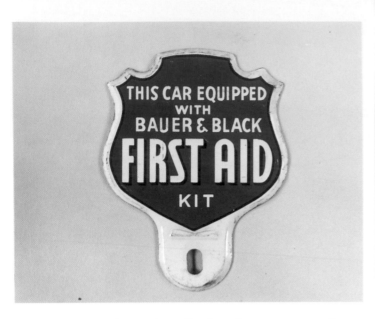

Fellow motorists know who to flag down in an emergency; Bauer & Black's First Aid tag attachment. 4⅞" x 3¾".

A bright crest from the Tarrant County Medical Society in Fort Worth, Texas. 5" x 3½".

The Southwest Motor Club from Fort Worth, Texas, manufactured this 4⅛" x 4⅝" tag.

It's as easy as the ABCs—Always Be Careful, says the Alemite Brigadiers Club. 5" x 6¾".

Pennzoil is for safety; a 4⅞" x 4½" reflector tag attachment.

"Long May It Wave," a rippling flag on a 4¼" x 3¼" tag ornament.

A badge ornament for officers of the North American Police and Sheriff's Association, 5¾″ x 4¼″.

Fleetwing Gasoline reminds drivers that "Safety Pays," with this 6″ x 4⅞″ tag attachment.

Lion advertises "Naturalube," their new motor oil product, on this 6″ x 6¼″ tag.

A golden eagle spreads its wings over a crest reminding drivers to remember Pearl Harbor. 5⅜″ x 4¾″.

Another Pearl Harbor memorial tag, in red, white and blue. 4⅜″ x 10″.

A 3″ x 10″ tag from a Mineral Wells, Texas, Lincoln-Mercury dealer.

"God Bless America" and a gently waving flag on this shield-shaped tag ornament, 5⅛″ x 3¼″.

Star Tires advertise on this 4⅛″ x 11″ tag attachment.

A tag from Heine & Goetz Motors, a Yoakum Plymouth/Dodge dealer. 2⅝″ x 10″.

A tag from the Ted Daly Motor Co., a Ford dealer in Palmer (state unknown). 3″ x 9⅞″.

A tag from a Kaiser-Frazer dealer in Fort Worth, Texas. 3⅜″ x 10″.

Ben Seyler's sales and service agency in Muenster, Texas advertises on this 4¾" x 9⅞" tag attachment.

From Rio Grande City, Texas, a tag from the Cavazos Motor Company. 3" x 9⅝".

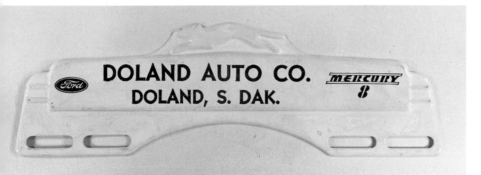

A South Dakota Mercury dealership advertises here, 3" x 9⅝".

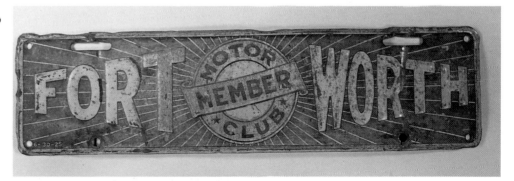

Fort Worth's Motor Club members displayed this 3½" x 13¼" tag ornament with pride.

A campaign tag, endorsing Hoover for President. 3" x 13⅝".

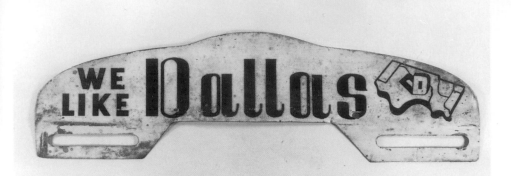

The famous Texas spirit seems lukewarm on this tag ornament, which reads "We like Dallas." 3" x 10".

A 1946 commemorative tag ornament from Fredericksburg, Texas, celebrating 100 years of Texas statehood. 4⅛" x 10".

A motor company's tag from Fort Worth, Texas. 3⅝" x 10".

A souvenir tag ornament from Mount Rushmore, 5½" x 11¼".

A repair garage advertises with tag ornaments in Austin, Texas. 3″ x 10″.

A D-X reflector, 4½″ x 3½″.

A Chevrolet dealership in Italy, Texas advertises here. 2⅞″ x 10″.

Sunoco Gasoline's patented tag attachment featured a monogram of the car owner's own initials. 5″ x 8″.

Picher, Oklahoma touts the world's largest zinc and lead field, on this license plate ornament, 5¾″ x 6¼″.

A reflector from Toledo Blade, 3″x 2″.

A souvenir tag from Hot Springs National Park in Arkansas. 5¾″ x 6¼″.

An En-Ar-Co reflector tag, 5⅞″ x 3¾″.

A "medical doctor" tag, 4″ x 4¼″.

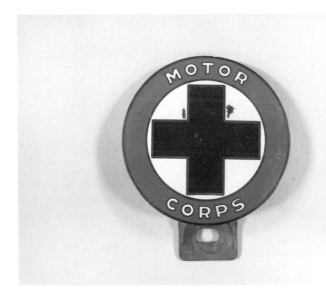

The red and green Motor Corps tag attachment, 4¼″ x 3½″.

A Knight bearing the shield "Co-operate" urges drivers to "save a life" by driving carefully. The Public Highway League in Brooklyn, New York produced this 8½″ x 5¾″ tag attachment in 1935.

A Phillips 66 tag, 6″ x 6″.

Nealco Antifreeze's mascot is bundled up on this license tag ornament, 6¾″ x 3¾″.

A Goodyear reflector tag from a town named "Surprise" in New York, 4⅞″ x 3½″.

A star-shaped reflector urging safety, 6⅞″ x 4¾″.

"Safety First," warns this yellow tag, 4¾″ x 3⅞″.

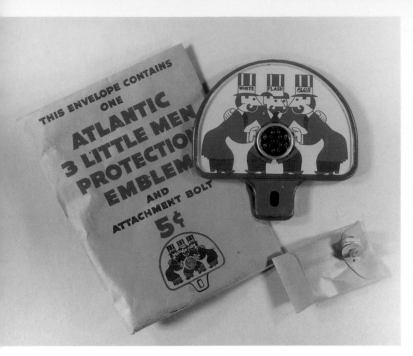

Atlantic's "3 Little Men" reflector tag attachment (4⅝" square) and its envelope packaging.

Tydol's very round service station attendant pursues customers, 4½" x 6⅝".

Fort Worth is where the West begins, says this cast aluminum tag, 3¼" x 10⅝".

A cast aluminum tag attachment from the Civil Air Patrol, 4⅛" x 10".

An advertising tag attachment, 3" x 10", from a Wisconsin Ford dealership.

Harrah's Club wants customers in Reno, even if they have to get there by mule! License tag ornament, 7″ x 12¼″.

A tag advertising Hollis Swift motor oil, 4⅛″ x 11⅛″.

A 3½″ x 10″ tag reads "Press."

Mobil's flying horse, 4½″ x 6¼″.

A different version of Mobil's flying horse, 4½″ x 6¼″.

The flying horse mascot for Mobil urges motorists to drive safely, 5⅜″ x 6⅜″.

Mobil's flying horse on a tag sponsoring the California World's Fair, 5⅜″ x 6″.

Another Mobile "Drive Safely," with a detailed, embossed flying horse. 5⅜″ x 6⅜″.

The Mobil horse flying over a red, white and blue "America First" motto, 5⅜″ x 6⅜″.

A wrench and a wheel, on a 1949 membership tag for railroad mechanics in a national organization. 6" x 4½".

A "corny" tag flies along, above the license plate of De Kalb motorists. 4¼" x 8⅜".

A political tag attachment calls for the repeal of the 18th Amendment, 2⅝" x 12".

A taxi tag from Boston, 4¼" x 4½".

Pemex Gasoline's travel club encourages trips to Mexico, on a 5" x 3⅛" tag.

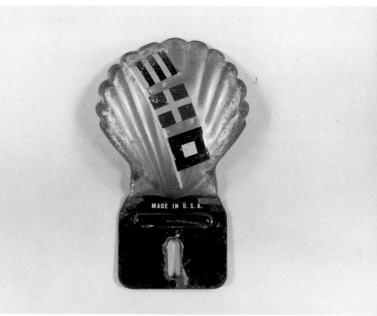

Shell Gasoline flags signal "I share the road," 5¼" x 3¼".

Blue Sunoco's lube cap, with a high-speed yellow streak.

Pennzoil has two lube caps, both urging motorists to sound their "Z"s.

Top: A fearsome snarl on a Wolf's Head lube cap; bottom: Conoco's green lube cap with red trim.

Top: Lube cap from Pure; bottom: Parapet Special Motor Oil's lube cap.

Top: RPM's lube cap makes ambitious promises; bottom: Pennzoil's lube cap guarantees safe lubrication and supreme quality from its Z-7 oil.

The dignified blue and orange, corded hat of a Gulf service station attendant.

Top: A lube cap from Quaker State Motor Oil; bottom: Royal Triton's "Finest"—a lube cap in kingly purple.

Top: Mobiloil's famous winged horse flies across this red lube cap; bottom: A lube cap from Texaco for Marfak.

Mobilgas/Mobiloil green, white and red beanie-cap.

Publicity buttons from the Gilmore Red Lion, the Filling Station Employees Union, and Socony Motor Gasoline, each an inch or smaller.

Shell's cheerfully literal station attendant badge, 2⅞" x 3½".

The Standard Oil Company of New York spreads the word on this 1" pin and this 3½" pocket mirror.

A snappy badge, 1¾" square, for Tydol employees to wear on their caps.

Mobiloil's advertisement for triple-action motor oil, on a 4" pin.

Cosden sold high octane gasoline to adults, but gave away for free these "Traffic Cop" badges, 1¾", for children.

Top (l-r): A 1941 ¾" pin from Chevrolet, advertising "the new style hit of "41," the Fleetline; a sly wink from Chevrolet, on this ¾" pin; "Stand By," signals Chevrolet on this ¾" pin; this 2⅜" dangling "Valve in Head" pin asserts that "Everybody Knows Buick."

Bottom (l-r): Ford's 1937-1938 oblong pin is ⅝" x 1"; this 1" pin announces that 1932 is "A Ford Year," especially for the V-84; this Indian-theme 1" pin promises that Pontiac is the "Chief of Value."

Conoco's 1⅝" x 2¼" station attendant name tag.

In the same pattern as Standard Oil's, Humble's 1¾" x 2⅞" attendant name tag.

Top: Standard Oil Company's curved cap badge, 1½" x 2⅞"; bottm: this name tag for Esso Service, 1½" x 2¼", waits to be filled out.

Standard Oil name tag. 1¾" x 2⅜".

Texaco went all out for their attendant name tags...this one, 1¾" x 2⅛", is flowered, feathered and starred.

Amoco's sharp, red and black enamel pin, 1¾" x 2¾".

For this 3⅛″ pin, Phillips 66 hired the first sign of spring to cheerfully remind customers to use their new summer oils.

Bottom left: Houston's Humble Oil and Refining Co. passed out this tiny hand mirror, 1¾″ x 2¾″. Esso and Esso Extra pins, both 1¾″ x 2¾″.

Cities' Service shining-eyed little boy smiled out from a 3½″ pin.

Veedol Motor Oil's 2½″ pin promises Supreme Quality.

One of Gulf's cap badges recognizing outstanding driving records.

Left: this 1¾″ pin marks the wearer as a member of the Phillips 66 Knot-Hole Gang; right: Goodyear takes first prize for this 1936 "Blue Ribbon Values" pin, 2″.

A Shell driver's award pin, 2″ in diameter.

Left: Gulf's powerhouse of a pin is 2″ in diameter; a 2½″ souvenir pin from the Gilmore Auto Races.

Delicately traced ribbons adorn Texaco's 1914, 1″ pin.

A contractor's tag, 1⅝″ x 2⅜″, from Socony Mobil in Buffalo, NY.

A Texaco uniform patch from the 1960s.

Uniform buttons from Texaco in the 1950s.

Pin-back buttons from Liberty Oil, Delco Battery, and American Gasoline.

ROAD MAPS

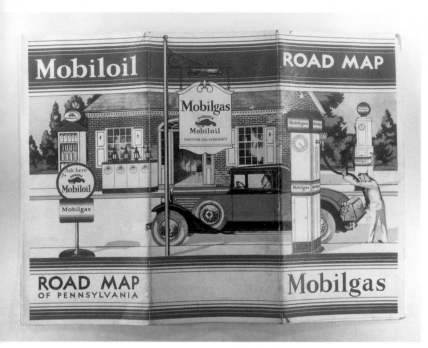

From 1932, Mobil's prettily illustrated map of Pennsylvania. The oil companies spared no expense in graphics, colors, or contrasts when it came to advertising their products. Some excellent examples of this were the road maps, oil cans and glass containers.

Marathon Oil Co., the "Best in the Long Run," produced this tri-color map of Arkansas, Kansas, Missouri, Oklahoma and Texas in 1934.

Conoco's lavishly printed Kansas road map, from 1920.

An edition of the "En-ar-co National News," distributed at National Refining Co. stations in 1928, features games, mysteries, cartoons and serial puzzles.

White Eagle's map of Kansas, with advertisements for their Balanced and Ethyl gasoline.

Texas Pacific Coal and Oil Co.'s dramatically illustrated map of highways and scenic tours, from 1934.

A tiny map of a huge state, this "midget" road map of Texas from the mid-1920s measures 2⅛″ x 3⅜″ folded, 9″ x 12″ unfolded.

Loreco (Louisiana Oil Refining Corporation) presented this nicely-illustrated map to Texas roads in 1929.

A Texas map from Marathon, 1934.

Arizona, from the Conoco Travel Bureau, 1933.

An Indiana map from Standard, 1940.

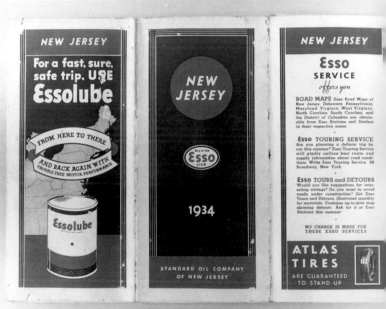

Flying geese on a Standard Oil Co. map of Indiana, 1934.

A guide to Sinclair-Trail comfort stations on the drive from Laredo, Texas to Mexico City, circa 1937.

Opposite page top right:
A map of the "Windy City," from Sinclair circa 1940.

Opposite page center right:
A 1934 New Jersey Map from Esso.

Phillips 66's map of Missouri, 1936.

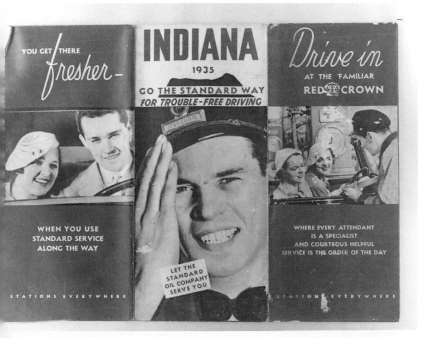

A courtesy map of Indiana from Red Crown, 1935.

A Barnsdall map of Kansas from 1937.

Sinclair's splashy, illustrated map of Kansas from 1934.

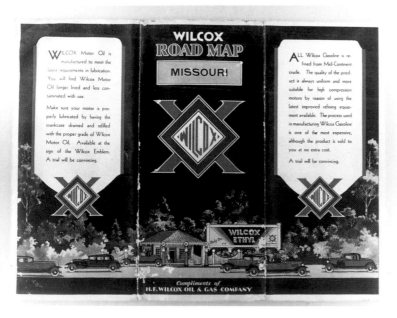

A map of Missouri from Wilcox Oil & Gas Co., 1933.

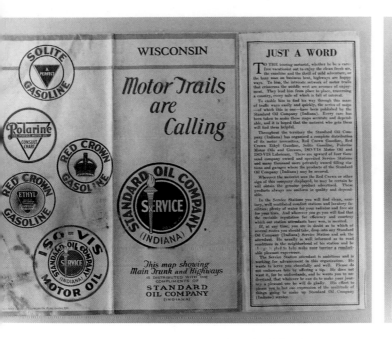

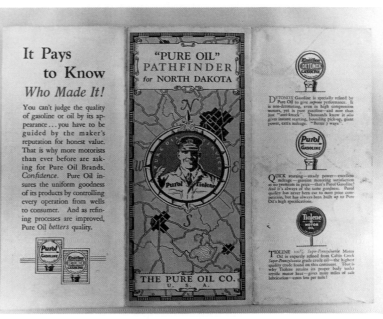

A highway map of Wisconsin from Standard Oil Co., 1927.

Pure Oil Co.'s Pathfinder for North Dakota, circa 1934.

Another brightly illustrated road map from Sinclair—Idaho, Montana and Wyoming from 1934.

A bird's eye view on this Sinclair road map of Texas from 1934.

Gulf's road map of Ohio from 1934.

A United States road map from Gulf, 1932.

Arizona, 1935, from the state's highway department.

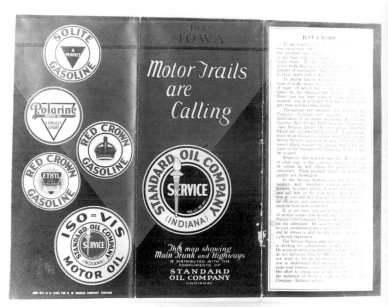

Standard's map of Iowa, 1929.

"Tydol Trails" through Pennsylvania and New Jersey, 1934.

A charmingly illustrated map of Illinois from Shell, 1933.

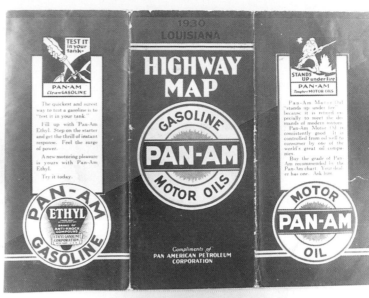

Pan Am's highway map of Louisiana from 1930.

Another Shell Illustrated map, Philadelphia, circa 1930.

"Trails of the Red Lion" on the Pacific Coast from Gilmore, 1930.

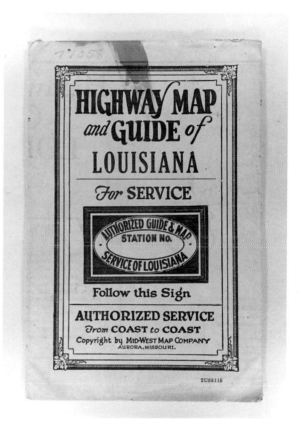

Mid-West Map Company's 1930 guide to Louisiana.

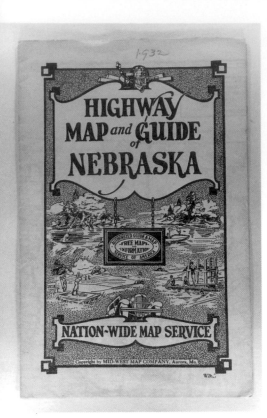

A 1932 map of Nebraska from the Mid-West Map Company.

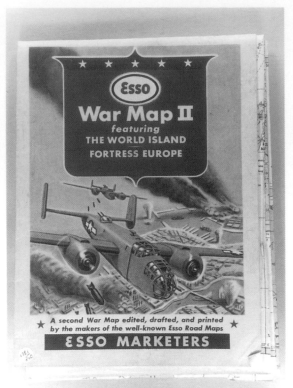

Esso's dramatic map of World War II Europe.

The AAA's Virginia seashore map, circa 1928.

A motor and resort guide from the Chicago Daily News, 160 pages, 1928.

AAA's road map of the U.S. transcontinental highway, 1932.

A 1916 tour book from Locke's guides travellers from El Paso, TX to Shreveport, LA.

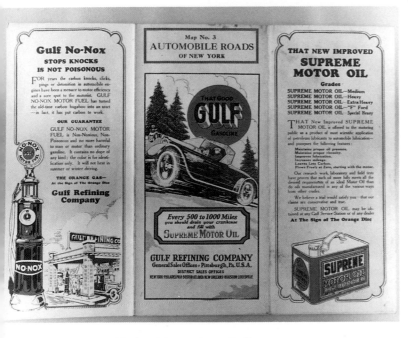

A 1933 New York road map from Gulf.

Cities Service's map of the Southwestern U.S., circa 1945.

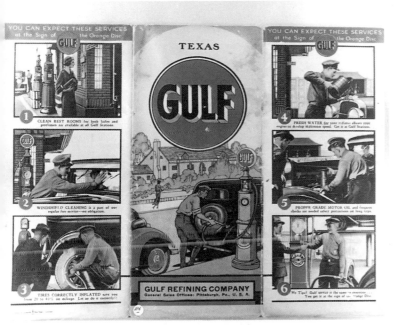

A Texas map from Gulf, 1933.

From 1925, a beautiful drivers' guide to touring Pike's Peak by car.

Socony's 1929 road map of New York.

An Ohio map from Shell, 1935.

A lovely souvenir map of Colorado Springs and Manitou (in the Pikes Peak region), circa 1925.

A 1934 road map of Minnesota from Texaco.

A Nebraska road map from Conoco, 1940.

A 1963 road map of New Jersey, from Mobil.

Atlanta White Flash's 1940 map of Pennsylvania/New Jersey.

Shell Oil Co.'s tour book of Route 66, from 1949.

A Texas road map from Sinclair, circa 1935.

Socony-Vacuum's map of New York state, 1935.

A 1931 map of Georgia from Standard Oil.

A 1930 map of Denver's sightseeing Gray Line.

A Conoco map of Wyoming from 1931.

A road map and historical guide to New Jersey from Sunoco, circa 1940.

A 1962 map of Fort Worth, from Conoco.

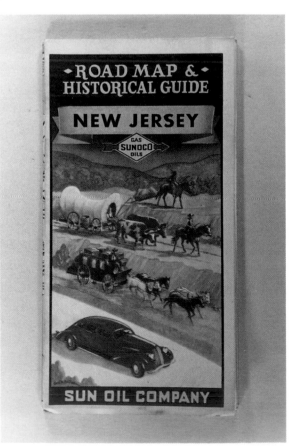

Sunoco's Pennsylvania map from 1940.

From 1950, a Texaco hanging map holder, 2¼" x 4" x 9" tall.

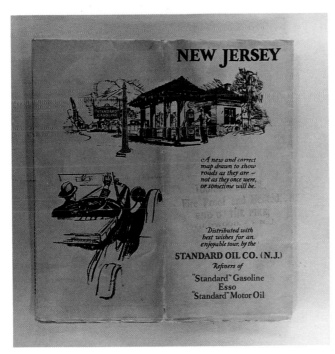

A New Jersey road map from Standard Oil in 1927.

A German map from Shell, circa 1935.

TRAVELLERS' NEEDS

A Magnolia first aid kit, circa 1935-1940. 4″ x 10″ diam.

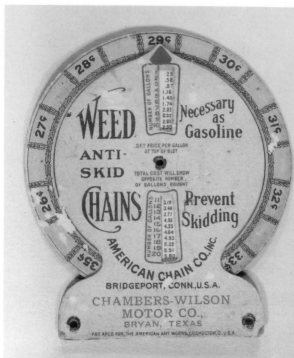

Weeds Chains mileage gauge chart wheel, 3″ diam.

A small (2¾″ x 3¼″) first aid kit from Mobil, circa 1945-1950.

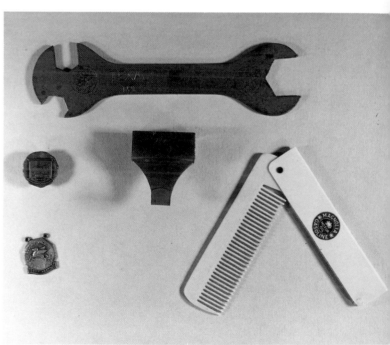

Various travelling supplies.

From 1935, a Phillips 66 first aid kit, 4¾″ x 8″ x 22″.

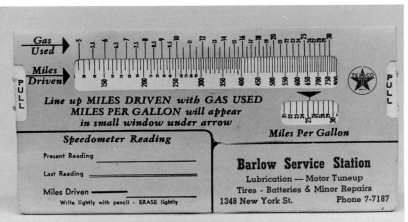

A mileage gauge from Texaco, circa 1950, 2⅞″ x 6″.

Shell give-away hat and coat hangers from the 1930s, 3¼″ long.

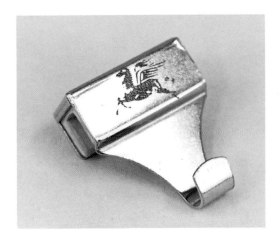

A Mobil clip clothes hanger for use over automobile windows, 1¼″ x 1½″, circa 1950.

Another Mobil clothes hanger, 1½″ x 2½″.

Paper-cased sewing kits from Phillips 66 and Shell.

Sewing kits with thimbles, 2″ long, from Gulf, Rio Grande and Cities Service.

A sewing kit from Buick, 1½″ x 2¼″, and an emery board kit from Humble, 1¾″ x 2¾″.

A needle kit from Lincoln, 2⅛″ x 3⅝″, and a travel set of razor blades from Texaco. Not Texaco Gasoline.

Keychains from Texaco, circa 1935-1945.

This Mobil keychain from 1955 holds two coins as well.

A Texaco watch fob from the 1920s.

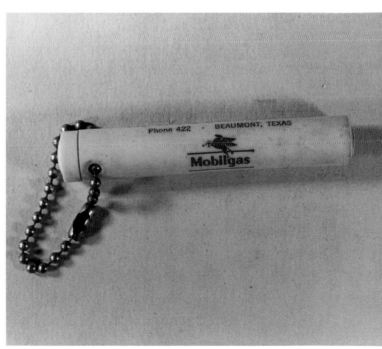

A Mobil keychain from 1945-1950, with space in the tube for storing a rolled-up drivers license.

A keyholder from Shell, circa 1970.

The Michelin Man key chain, circa 1970.

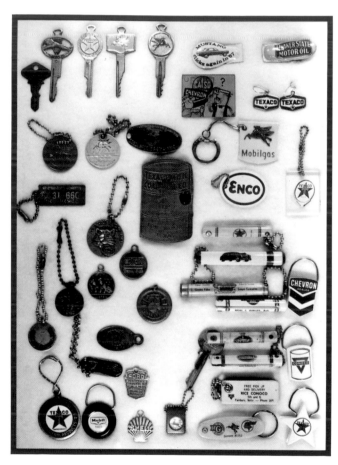

A wide array of keys and keychains.

Key from a 1925 Model "T" Ford and a 1930 Chrysler, and keys stamped by Texaco and Mobil (1950), Mobil and Pure (1965).

A Deep Rock 1-gallon gasoline can from Chicago.

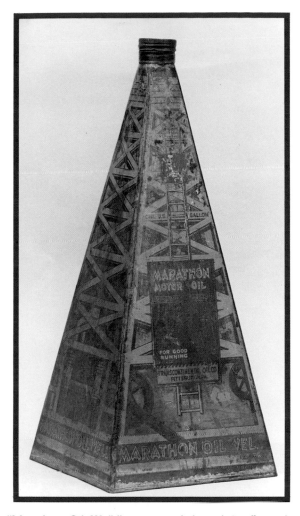

The "Marathon Oil Well," a pyramid-shaped 1-gallon oil can stands 15½" high from a 6½" base.

The Marathon logo decorates this 5-gallon motor oil can.

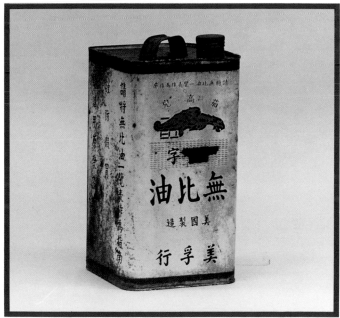

From Japan, this "Gargoyle" oil tin by Mobil holds 5 quarts.

Another "Gargoyle" motor oil tin from Mobile, this one meant for their Arctic Special oil, and printed in Arabic.

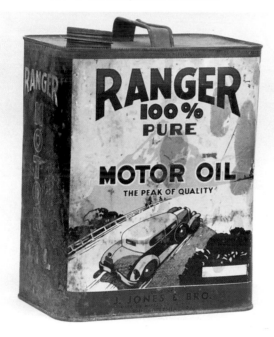

From approximately 1938, a 5-gallon can for Hudson motor oil.

From Philadelphia, a 2-gallon, illustrated can for Ranger motor oil.

A display of 15 Texaco tins, including ones for axle grease, liquid was dressing and home lubricant oil.

A Gamage 5-gallon can (20½" x 10" x 10"), lavishly illustrated with a racing boat, sea-spray and open sky on one panel...

...with a racing roadster on another, and with a swooping hydroplane on a third.

Oilzum's motor oil can holds 5 quarts.

Left: A quart bottle for motor oil from Pennzoil, 10" tall.

Right: From Esso, a 12¼" tall motor oil bottle.

From Shell, a hand-soldered metal 1-gallon oil can, with an embossed shell emblem.

Two 5-quart cans of Sinclair motor oil.

A tin 5-quart can for Mobiloil's Arctic Medium Gargoyle motor oil, in English.

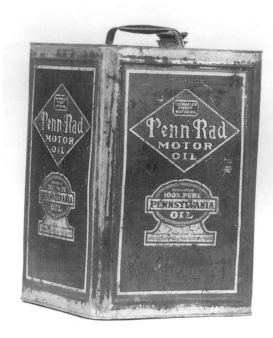

Penn Rad motor oil's 5-gallon can.

A can for Canadian Imperial motor oil from En-Ar-Co, 1 qt.

A tin container for Mobiloil's Light-Medium Body Arctic Gargoyle motor oil, 5 quarts, printing in English.

A 5-gallon can for Mobiloil's Heavy Gargoyle motor oil, in English.

A 2-gallon can for Mobil's Lubrite motor oil.

A 5-quart tin for Mobiloil's "E" series Gargoyle motor oil, "especially recommended for Ford Cars."

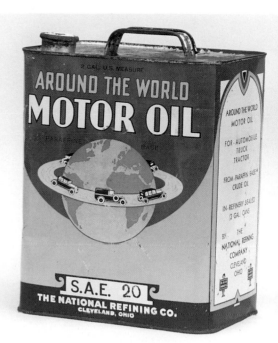

Left:
In Spanish, a 5-quart tin container for Mobiloil's Gargoyle Arctic "Fluido" motor oil.

Right:
National Refining Co.'s "Around the World" motor oil, two gallon can.

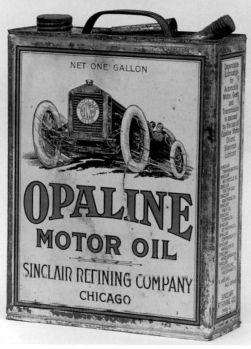

Mobiloil's tin for Gargoyle "A" heavy-medium motor oil, printing in Swedish.

A gallon can of Opaline Motor Oil.

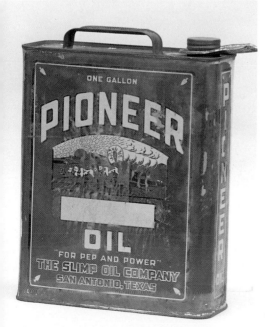

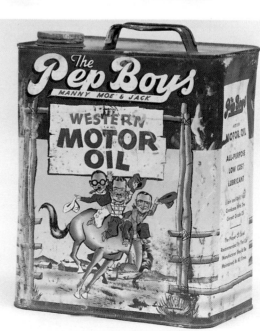

Above right:
Defender Motor Oil, from Philadelphia, in a 2 gallon can.

Right:
A two gallon can for Western Motor Oil from The Pep Boys, illustrated with their usual whimsy.

Left:
A 1-gallon can for Slimp Oil Company's "Pioneer" oil, from San Antonio, TX.

A two gallon can for Empire State motor oil.

A five gallon can for Sears' Cross Country motor oil.

Aero Eastern's motor oil can (2 gallons) guarantees 2500 miles with their super refined oil.

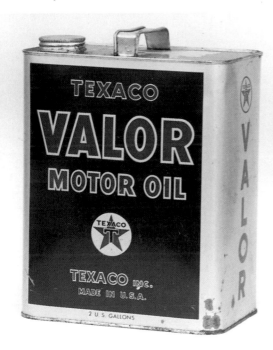

Texaco's Valor motor oil can, 2 gallons.

A Gulf can for Gulfpride oil, 5 gallons.

OIL CHANGE REMINDERS

This Mobil blotter from the 1930s gives car owners a strong warning.

These oil change reminders range from 1¼" to 2" wide.

Another set of oil change reminders.

Oil change reminder tags from Humble, Linco, Ace High and Phillips 66.

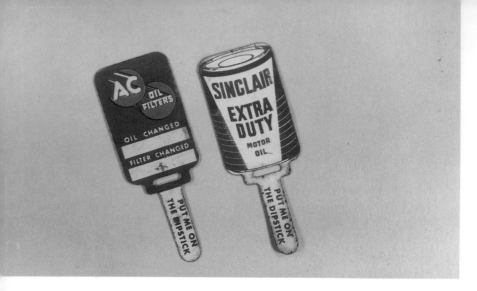

These tags had their tabs bent onto the oil tank dipsticks. 1¼" x 3¼".

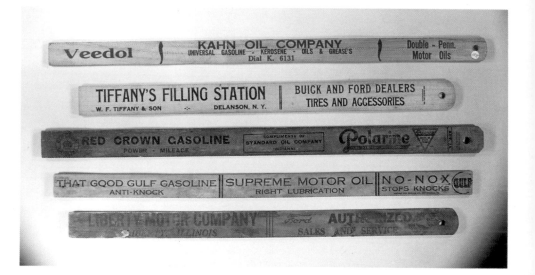

Sticks for checking oil or fuel levels, from 1900 to 1925, 14" to 17" long.

A packet of lubrication stickers from the 1950s, 1½" x 6½".

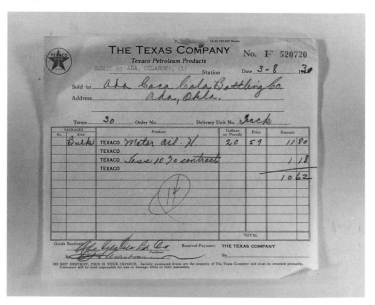

Coca Cola bottlers in Oklahoma got a pretty good deal, according this Texaco invoice from 1930.

PRODUCTS FOR SERVICE STATIONS

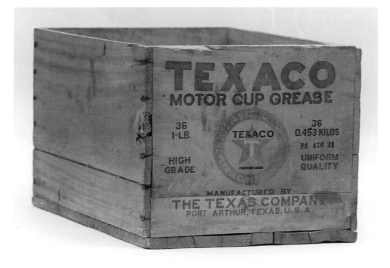

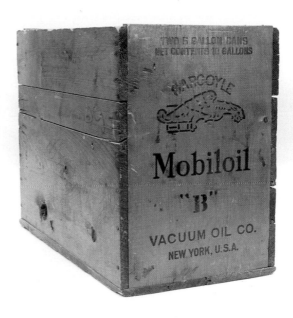

A wooden crate for motor cup oil at Texaco stations, circa 1925. 15¼" x 10½" x 17".

A wooden crate from Mobil, circa 1925.

Texaco's wooden crate for transmission lubricant, 10½" x 11", circa 1915.

A service-oriented light switch plate from Humble station rest rooms in the 1950s.

A Humble response-box, 6" long, from the 1960s.

A Socony rest room soap dispenser, 4½″ diam., from the 1930s.

From Mobil, bottles for Upperlube and Hand Lotion, both 4¼″ tall.

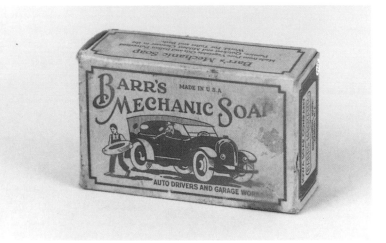

Barr's Mechanic Soap, from the 1920s.

A coupon book from Conoco, 2¼″ x 5⅛″, from the 1950s.

Mother Penn gasoline coupons, 2¼″ x 5″, from the 1930s.

LAMPS AND OTHER REPLACEMENT PRODUCTS

Boxed automobile lamp kits from The Pep Boys. 2⅝″ x 4½″ on the right, 2⅝″ x 3⅝″ on the left.

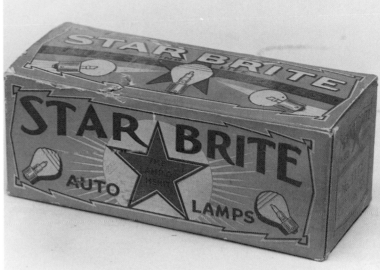

A colorful box for Star Brite's auto "lamps of merit."

Westinghouse's miniature Mazda lamps, 2.5 volts.

Edison's Mazda lamps in their zippy yellow "handy kits for your car," 2⅝″ x 3⅝″.

Car bulb kits in tin canisters from Osram and from Royal Ediswam.

An emergency bulb and fuse kit for Ford drivers.

A more extensive emergency kit from Ford, including a spark plug, a tail lamp bulb, two head lamp bulbs, and a tire repair kit.

Left: the Wizard Auto Bulb Kit tells drivers to "Carry a Spare," 2⅝" x 3⅝"; right: Stop! says Safety Lites package. "Keep Within the Law" with properly functioning head lamps, inside this 2⅝" x 3⅝" tin.

Left: Eveready's Mazda automotive lamp kit comes in a 1½" diam., 4½" long cylindrical canister; right: a Mazda Auto Lamp from National, 1⅝" x 3½".

A capsule-shaped car lamp kit from Eveready.

A Westinghouse bulb tin, 2⅝" x 3⅝" and a Mazda Bulb tin, 2⅝" x 4", from General Electric.

An early headlight bulb from Hi-lite.

Three kits from Westinghouse: an auto lamp tin, 2⅞" x 2⅞"; a Mazda bulb tin, 2⅝" x 3⅝"; and an emergency bulb tin, 2⅝" x 3¾".

A "genuine" lamp bulb kit from Chevrolet, 2⅝" x 3¾".

CAR CARE PRODUCTS

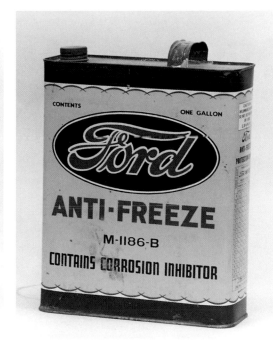

Three products from Whiz: A 1-pint canister of auto top dressing, 1⅞″ x 3⅞″ x 5¼″; 1/2-pint metal polish, diameter 2⅜″ x 4½″; a 1-quart can of polish, diameter 3½″ x 7½″.

The front view of a 1-gallon can of Ford's anti-freeze.

The rear view of Ford's anti-freeze.

Dallas' "Speedoline" was said to increase gasoline mileage for motorists. 2¾″ x 4¼″ x 7⅛″.

A 1-pint can of Royal Saxon Auto Body Polish.

A tube of Wolf's Head "Door Ease" lubricant, 1″ x 4½″.

One quart of Blue Ribbon cream metal polish.

This two-part can held a total of 41 oz. of Kar B out tune-up fluid.

A store display for Gulfoil polish, 4½″ x 10″ x 11¾″.

Red Top (5⅛″ x 1⅞″) and Crown (4¼″ x 2⅝″).

From Veedol motor oil, an electric lighted display can, five-quart size, topped by a one-pound grease tin.

A display dispenser for spark plug gaskets.

Eveready Prestone anti-freeze cans, in 1-gallon and ½-gallon sizes.

Cans from Whiz, both 2″ x 3″. Powdered car wash and "Quik-seal" for radiator leaks.

Mobil's 1-quart motor oil jar, and a 2-lb. gear lube tin.

A 1-quart tin for Mobil's Gargoyle oil and, from Gilmore, a 1-lb. can of lubricant.

A selection of door-ease lubricants, all 1″ x 4½″, from Kendall, Pennzoil, Shell and Mobil.

A collection of nine Sears' Cross Country tins, including solder, valve-grinding compound, a tube repair kit, touch-up enamel, water-pump grease and other automotive products.

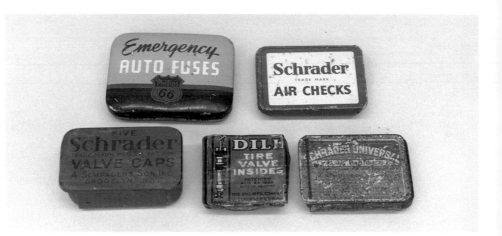

An assortment of repair kit tins: Emergency auto fuses from Phillips 66, tire valve insides from Dill, and Schrader's air checks, valve caps and valve insides.

A bucket advertising Firestone repair and replacement products, including tires, tubes, spark plugs, brake lining, rims, and accessories.

4¼" x 1¾" tins of Simoniz wax and "Kleener."

PATCH KITS

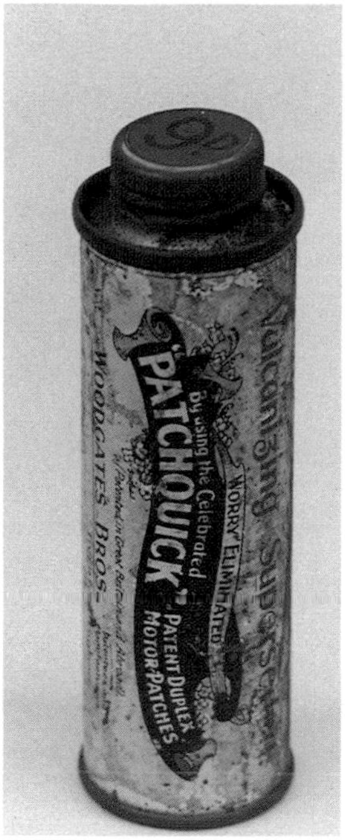

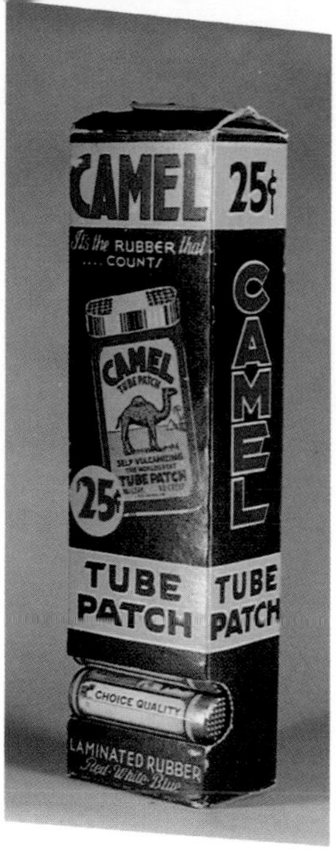

A Patchquick patch kit, 1¼" x 4".

A Camel Patch Kit display, 3⅝" x 13¼".

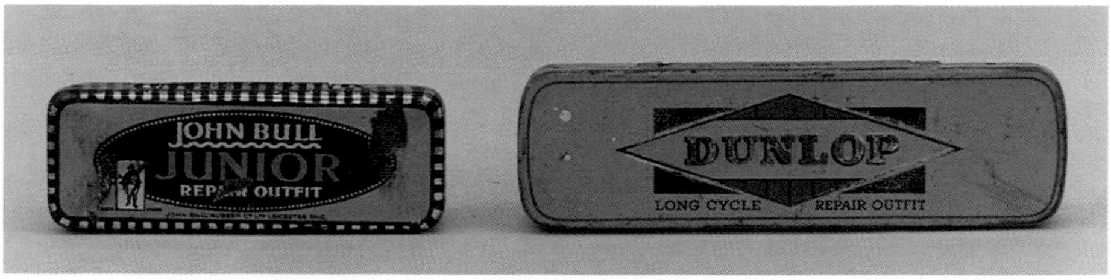

John Bull's patch kit, 1⅛" x 3¼", and Dunlop's, 1½" x 4½".

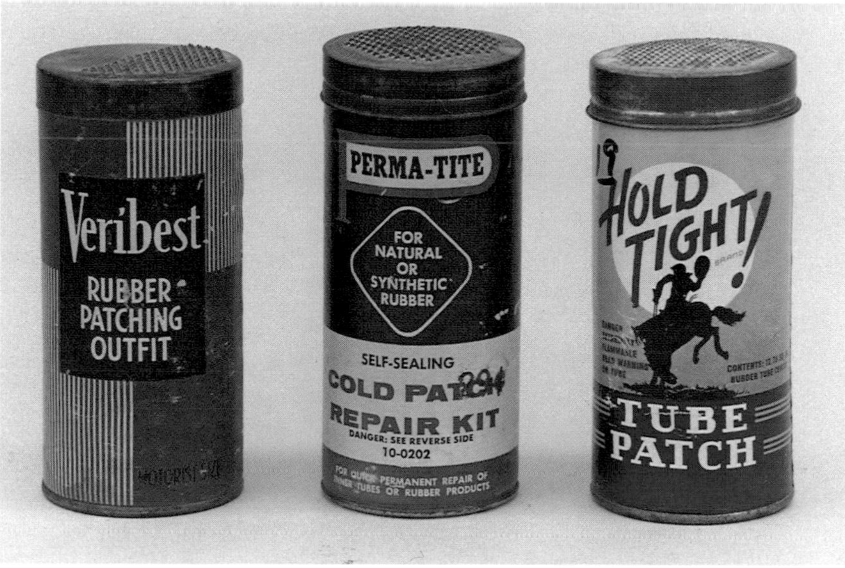

Veribest, Perma-tite, and Hold Tight's tire patch kits: 2" x 4¼", 2" x 4½", and 2" x 4⅜".

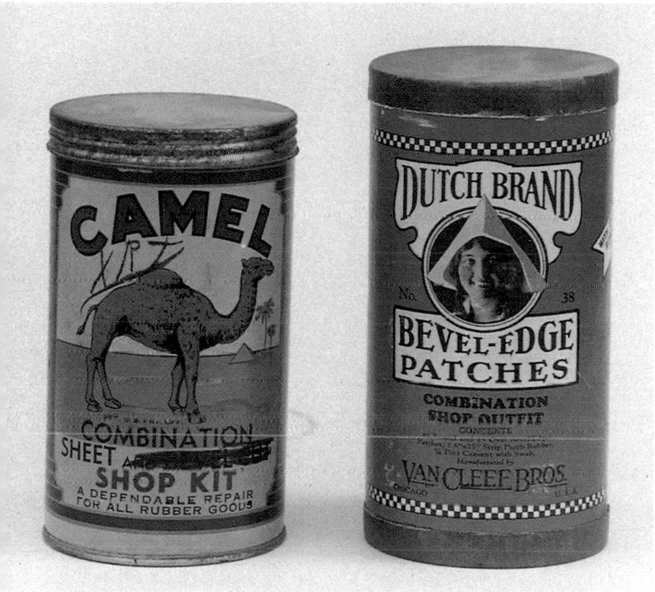

Patch kits from Camel, 3¾" x 6⅝", and Dutch, 3⅝" x 7⅜".

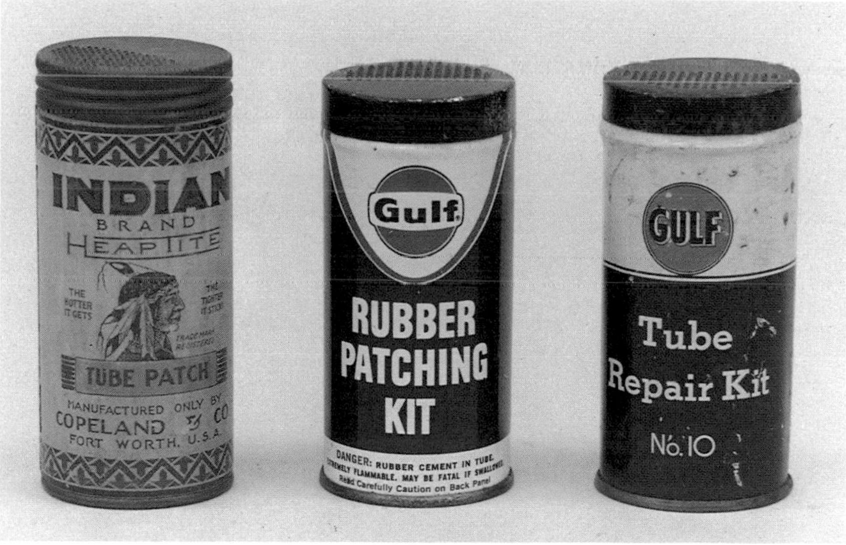

Patch kits from Indian, 2" x 4½", and Gulf, 2" x 4⅛" and 2" x 4¼".

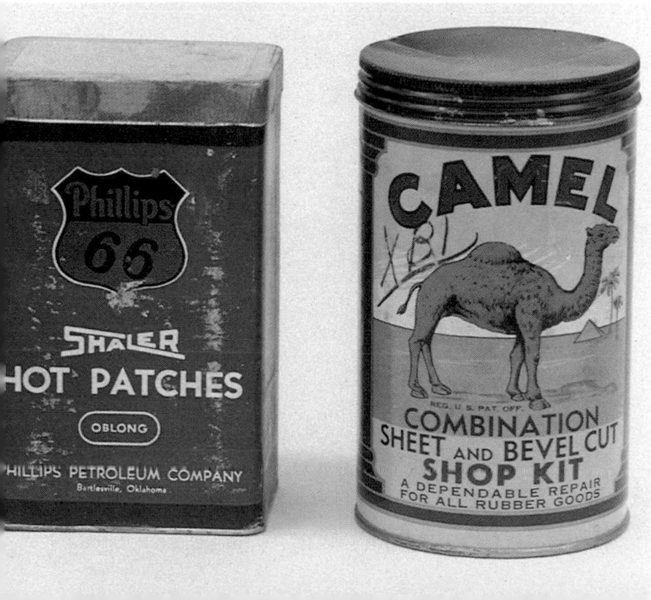

A Phillips 66 patch kit, 3⅞" x 6⅜", and another from Camel, 3¾" x 6⅝".

Patch kits made by Gross, 2" x 3⅞", Better, 2" x 4½", and Ford, 1¼" x 3½".

A Ford Model "T" patch kit, 3" x 6⅛".

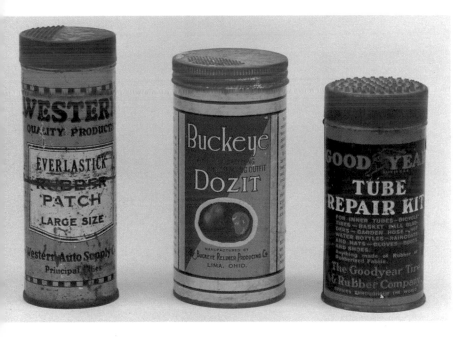

Western Auto, Buckeye and Goodyear patch kits, 2" x 5⅝", 2⅜" x 5" and 2⅛" x 4½".

Royal's patch kit, 2" x 4⅛", Ace's and Crest's, each 2" x 4⅜".

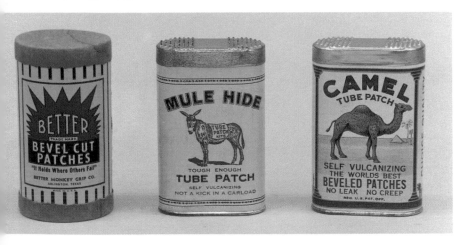

Better's patch kit, 2" x 3⅝", and kits from Mule Hide and Camel, each 2¼" x 3½".

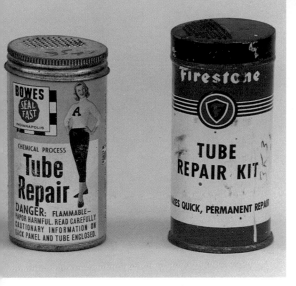

Kelly and Firestone patch kits, both 2″ x 4¼″, and one by Bowes, 1⅞″ x 3⅞″.

Lee patch kits, 2″ x 3½″ and 2″ x 4⅜″, and a Las-stik kit, 2″ x 4¼″.

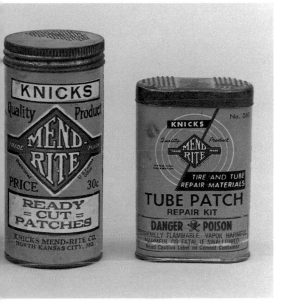

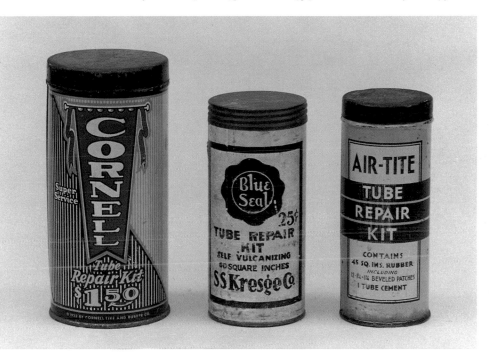

Gross's bevel-cut patches, 3¼″ x 4¼″; Mend-rite's, 2″ x 4⅜″ and 2¼″ x 3½″.

Patch kits from Cornell, 3″ x 6½″, Blue Seal, 2½″ x 6½″ and Air-Tite, 2¼″ x 5⅝″.

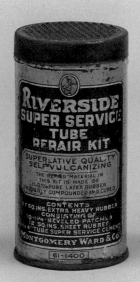

Hodgman, 1⅞″ x 5¼″, Riverside, 2¼″ x 4½″ and Many Miles, 2⅛″ x 4½″.

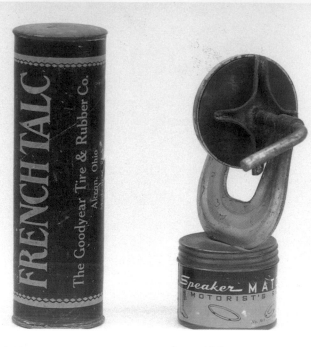

A Pullman patch kit, 2″ x 4¾″, a True Value, 2″ x 4⅜″, and a Firestone, 2″ x 4½″.

French Talc for tire tubes from Goodyear, 2⅛″ x 6¾″, and Speaker's patch kit and tube clamp, 6¼″ tall.

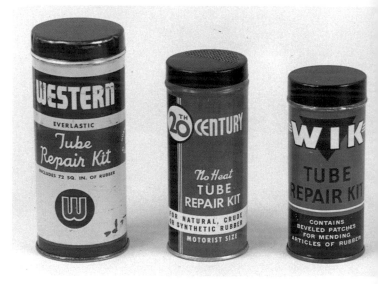

Patch kits from Lee, 2½″ x 5½″, Cross Country, 2¼″ x 5⅝″, and Phillips 66, 2¼″ x 5½.

Patch kits from Western, 2¼″ x 5½″, 20th Century, 2″ x 4¾″, and Wik, 1⅞″ x 4½″.

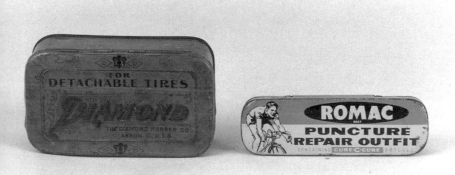

Diamond's patch kit, 2⅝″ x 4½″, and Romac's, 1½″ x 4½″.

Cross Country's patch kit, 2¼″ x 5⅝″.

A Richfield patch kit, 3½" x 9¼".

Patch kits from Lee, 2⅜" x 5½", U.S. Royal, 2¼" x 5", and Sturdee, 2½" x 5½".

Patch kits made by Sears, 2" x 4⅛", Whiz, 2" x 4½" and Goodyear, 2⅛" x 4⅝".

A patch kit form Allstate, 3' x 3½", and one from Peerless, 1⅞" x 4½".

Two Belnord patch kits, 3⅛" x 6" and 2¼" x 5½".

A patch kit from Fisk, 3" x 5".

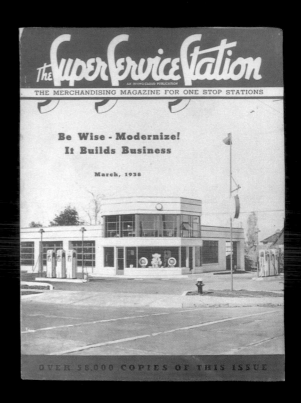

The *Super Service Station* magazine from January, 1938...

...and from March.

Super Service Station magazine's handbook for building profitable station business.

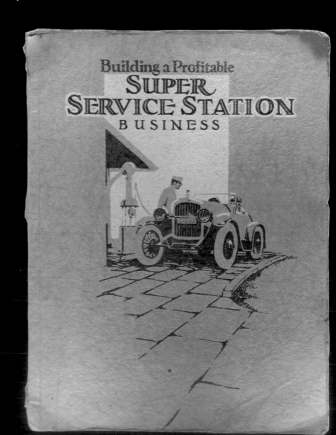

...from February...

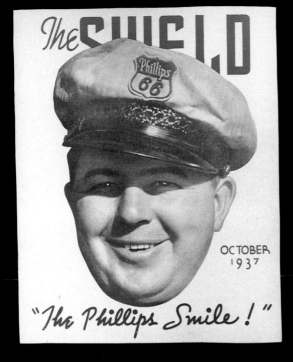

Phillips 66's monthly October, 1937 of their monthly magazine, *The Shield*.

The Texaco company magazine, 7½" x 10", from November of 1925.

Phillips' January, 1938 edition, starting the New Year with the marketing theme "Selling Sixty-Six."

Vacuum Oil's New Year edition of their *Gargoyle* magazine, 1926.

A powerhouse cover for June, 1935's *Auto-mobile Trade Journal*.

The 75th Anniversary edition of Texaco's company magazine *The Marketer*, 8½" x 11" from 1977.

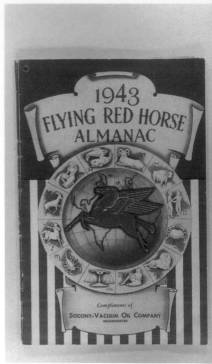

Socony-Vacuum's 1943 *Flying Red Horse Almanac*, 5½" x 8½".

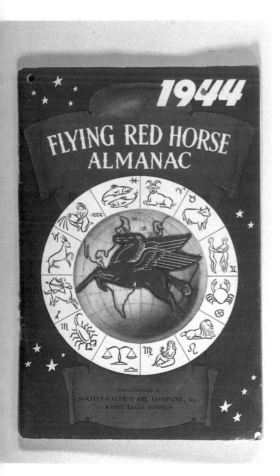

The 1944 *Flying Red Horse Almanac*.

A restfully-illustrated 1922-1923 *Stanolind Almanac* from Standard, 5½" x 8".

Stanolind's cheerful 1924-1925 almanac.

The Handbook for Service Station Salesmen, from Mobiloil, front view...

A U.S. government education manual on running service stations, written for military personnel.

...and back view.

A "Texan" pump catalog from 1933, 8½" x 11".

A Gulf car care manual, 3¼" x 6¼", inside...　　...and out.

This Wayne Pump mail-out catalog opens up to 18" x 24".

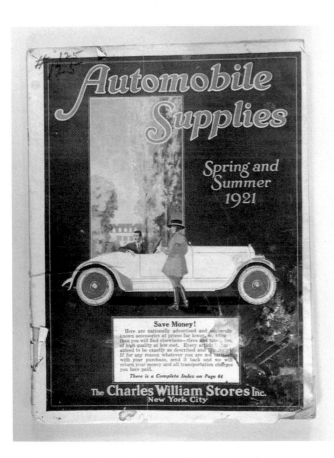

An auto supply catalog from 1921, 8½" x 11".

A 1927-1928 catalog from Fleckenstein Visible Pumps...

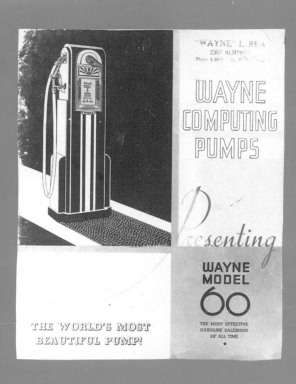

Covers for two 1935 catalogs, 8½″ x 11″, advertising Wayne's
Model 60—"The World's Most Beautiful Pump!"

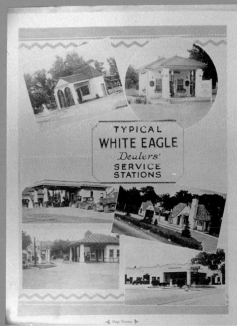

A "typical" page spread from inside the White Eagle catalog.

The embossed cover of a White Eagle catalog.

GAUGES

An assortment of tire gauges from the 1930s.

A green Schrader valve and air gauge display from the 1920s, 26″ tall.

A smaller, red valve display from Schrader, 14¾″ tall, from the 1920/30s.

The red Schrader display, opened at the back.

The green Schrader display, opened at the back.

PRODUCTS FOR THE HOME

Gulf's Electric Motor Oil in a glass bottle; a metal can of Gulfoil household lubricant; Phillips 66's Handy Household Oil.

A set of Texaco home lubricants.

Oiler cans from Marathon, Sinclair and Mobil.

Mobil's household lubricant in a handy oiler can.

All-purpose machinery oil for the home from Humble, Conoco and Sunoco.

Mobil Socony-Vacuum tin for moth crystals, and another for Lustre furniture polishing cloth.

Household oils in cans from Pure, Sohio, and Veedol.

Lighter fluid bottles from Gulf and Shell, with special holiday packaging from Sinclair.

A one-quart can of floor dressing from Magnolia Petroleum.

Box for outboard motor gear lubricant from Texaco, circa 1950.

HOUSEWARES

A 1950s kitchen towel, 16" x 29½", from Texaco.

A glass jar from Delco, 6½" x 7½" x 11½" tall.

A 1920s telephone directory from Eastern Avenue Tire Worls, 3½" x 16".

Radios in the shape of batteries from Atlas, Texaco and Phillips 66. 3¾" x 2¾" x 3¾" tall.

Radios in the shapes of various auto products, circa 1965-1970. All approximately 4" tall.

A tape measure from Humble, 2" x 2", circa 1950.

A Mobile drinking glass from 1966, 5″ tall.

A celluloid memo pad, circa 1910-1915, from Texaco (1¾″ x 3¾″) and a 6″ ruler from Ford, circa 1935.

A pocket mirror from Harry's Tire Service, 3⅜″ diam, circa 1915.

A free gift from Marathon to its customers in the 1950s, a 1⅜″ x 2½″ pot scrubber.

A ruler with its leather case from Magnolia, 8″, circa 1920.

A Sinclair glass coaster, 3¼″ diam., and an RPM lens tissue kit, 2½″ x 3⅝″.

"Gulfwax" paraffin, 2⅝″ x 5⅛″.

Magnolia wax and Texaco Texwax, 2½″ x 2½″ x 5⅛″.

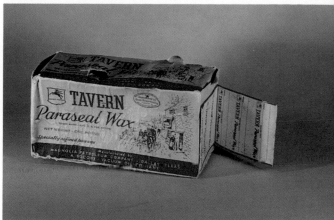

"Paraseal Wax," Tavern brand, from Movil, 2½″ x 2½″ x 5⅛″.

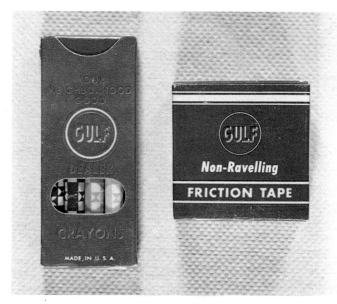

1950s give-away crayons (1½″ x 3¾″) from Gulf, and friction tape (2⅛″ x 2⅛″) from the 1960s.

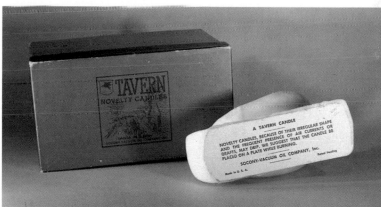

Socony-Vacuum (Mobil) Santa Claus candle for the holidays. 5″ long.

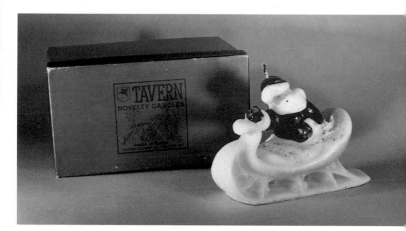

The label on the Santa candle's base.

Snowman candles from Socony-Vacuum (Mobil), 3″ tall.

Sinclair and Texaco thimbles, circa 1955-1965.

A 1920s needle-threader from Magnolia Gasoline.

Plastic bottle caps from Texaco, Mobil in the 1960s.

The Texaco anniversary lamp, 1977.

A set of give-away Shell coasters, from the 1960s.

An Independent Gasoline metal cup.

Bottle caps, an ashtray, a bottle top from Mobil, along with a name tag.

"FASHION" EYEWEAR

Give-away sunglasses from Ford, 1957.

A Wilson goggle tin, 2″ x 5⅜″, circa 1905.

A goggle tin from Cesgowide from 1905, 2⅛″ x 3¼″.

3-D glasses from Chrysler for the 1939 World's Fair. 2¾″ x 5″.

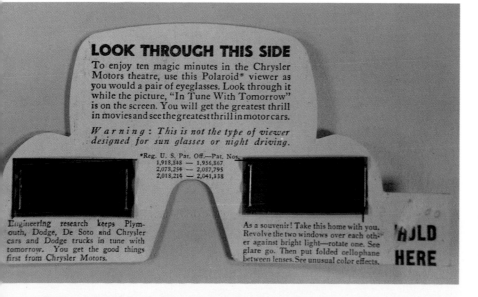

The reverse side of Chrysler's 3-D glasses, 1939.

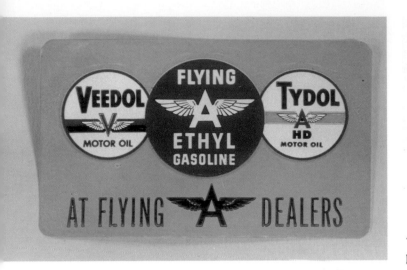

A combination billfold/calendar card from Flying "A", 2¼" x 3¾", 1952.

A Texaco watch fob, circa 1915-1920.

From Hartford Cord Tires in the 1930s, this personal baseball scorekeeper is 2⅜" diam.

A rain gauge from Esso, 5⅜" x 6½" from the 1960s.

From the 1930s, a filling station Christmas tree ornament, to be filled with candy. 1¾" x 6".

A 1930s tie clip from Texaco.

An assortment of logo items.

A model of the Michelin Man, 13¾″ tall.

Left: A give-away change purse from Mobil, 2¾″ x 2⅞″; top right: a Mobil flying horse fishhook; bottom right: a flying horse necklace or bracelet charm from Mobil.

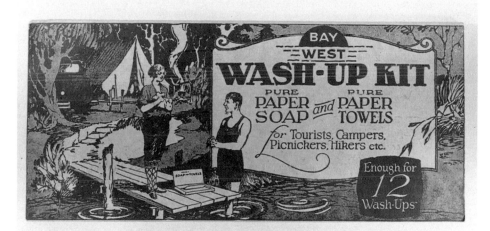

A soap and towel wash-up kit from the early 1920s, 5½″ x 12¼″.

Two belt buckles from Mobil.

THE WASH-UP KIT CONTAINS
SOAP AND TOWELS
Enough for 12 Complete Emergency Wash-Ups

THE SOAP PAPER	These and Water, all You Need	THE PAPER TOWELS
is made of a new combination of pure sulphate wood fibre and pure cocoanut oil soap.		are the famous Bay West Folded Dubltowls—the strongest made. They are instantly absorbent and lintless.

DIRECTIONS FOR USE

Hold one sheet of soap paper open in your hand. Dip paper and hands in water. Rub paper between hands. Rich lather develops at once. Continue to hold in hands and use like a soaped wash-cloth without dipping again until you are through lathering. Will not break up in hands and can be disposed of in one piece.

Use the towels as they come from Wash-Up Kit—two sheets together. These are the strongest paper towels ever made and may be used the same as cloth towels. May be dried and re-used if desired. May be used on the most sensitive skin without hesitation. Soft, refreshing and completely sanitary.

NO WET SOAP TO CARRY   **NO CLOTH TOWELS TO WASH**

The reverse of the Bay West wash-up kit.

A promotional paper mask from Chevrolet, 8¾″ x 11″, 1939.

From Texaco, a signed 12″ x 14½″ Ed Wynn mask from 1934.

A 20″ metal turn signal arm with mirror, circa 1930.

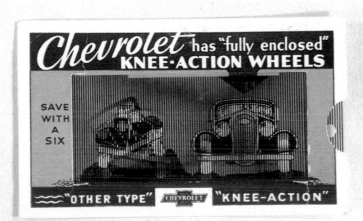

An animated advertising card from Chevrolet in the early 1930s, 2¼″ x 3¾″.

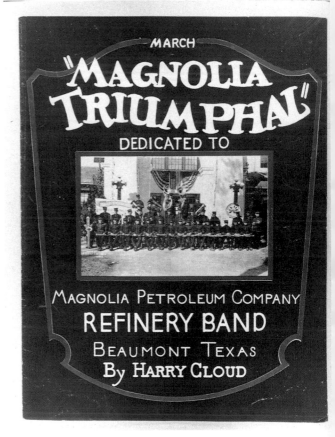

Sheet music from Magnolia, circa 1920.

SMOKING PARAPHERNALIA

This 4⅜" "Men at Work" ashtray from the '40s implied that no one could resist staring at the superior lines of a Buick.

A Ford cigarette tin, circa 1920.

Jenney Aero Gasoline used every inch of advertising space on this 4⅛" spinning ashtray game from the 1930s.

One Texaco station's promotional glass ashtray, 5¼" across.

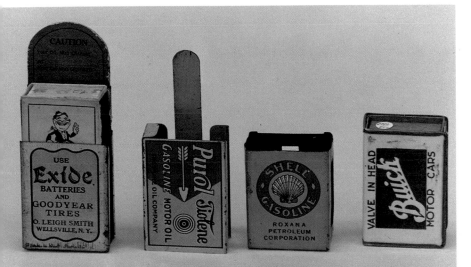

Left to right: In an era of smoking glamour, stations produced promotional items like this Exide/Goodyear match safe, which held one box of small wooden matches; Pural Tiolene's brightly-colored match safe; Shell Gasoline's sea shell logo, on a metal match safe; Buick advertised its motor cars on match safes.

LIGHTER FLUID DISPENSERS

A Shell lighter fluid dispenser, 19½″ x 5⅞″.

A detail of a Shell lighter fluid dispenser above, with the warning, "Petroleum Spirit Highly Flammable."

The "Bluebird" metal lighter fluid dispenser, 13⅜″ tall. One of the most ingenious uses for the old gas pump replica was to dispense lighter fluid. By inserting a coin into the gas pump, the pump dispensed enough fluid to fill a cigarette lighter.

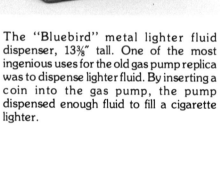

Shell's lighter fluid dispenser, a model of a gasoline pump, is 13″ tall.

A charming brass lighter fluid dispenser labelled "Dayton Pump Co. for Kuppenheimer Good Clothes," 10⅝″ x 6″.

A six-sided, locked lighter fluid dispenser from Van Lansing, 18″ x 7⅝″ of metal

Identical in style to Van Lansing's lighter fluid dispenser, but made of unpainted metal, this one is for "Van Lite," 18¾″ x 7½″.

Nasco's lighter fluid dispenser, 17½″ x 5″ of cast iron, is very heavy.

An Oronite lighter fluid dispenser, 15½″ x 5¾″, made of lithographed tin.

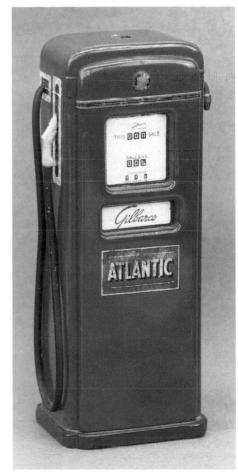

Gilbarro's wooden lighter fluid dispenser, a detailed model of a gas station pump, is 10″ tall.

FANS

A fan fit for a mermaid: Shell's 8½″ promotional paper fan.

The Phillips 66 logo on a paper fan in the shape of a highway sign, 8¾″.

This light-hearted illustrated paper fan reminds motorists to "Drive with Care." 7¾″ across, it circulated in the late 1920s and early 1930s.

A restful, quiet scene decorates Skelly Oil Company's promotional paper fan, which opens to 12¾″.

BOOKS

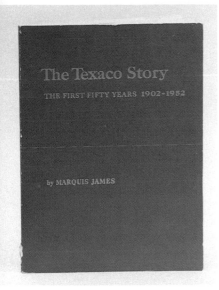

Texaco's fifty-year history, 8" x 11", published in 1952.

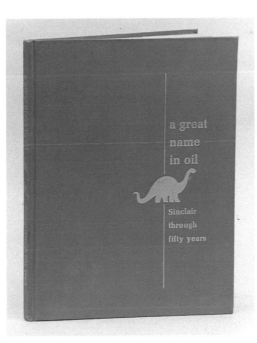

Sinclair published its own 50th anniversary company history.

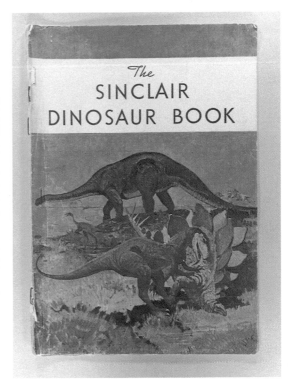

A give-away book about dinosaurs from Sinclair, 6¾" x 9¾".

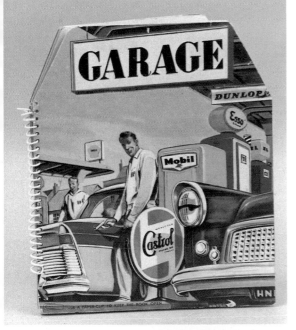

The cover of a service station pop-up book from England in the 1960s...

A mobilgas booklet about the history of Texas, 5¼" x 7¼".

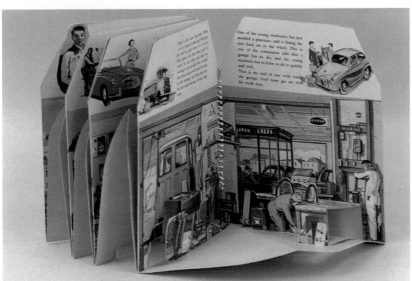

...and its bright, busy insides.

LOGS AND NOTEPADS

A souvenir calendar from Mobil, promoting their Magnolia tour of the Southwest. 14″ x 23″.

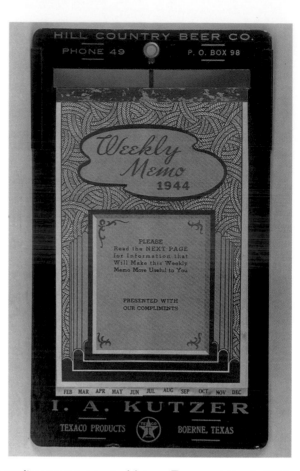

A complimentary memo pad from a Texaco station in 1944.

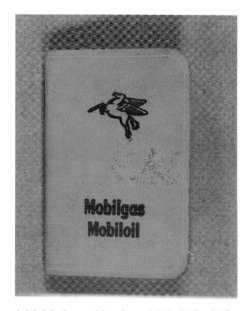

A Mobiloil travel log from 1951, 2⅛″ x 3¼″.

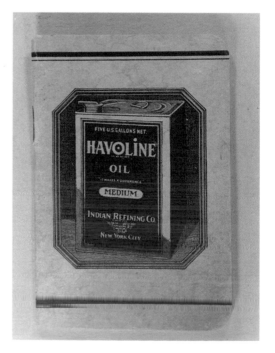

An auto log notebook from Havoline.

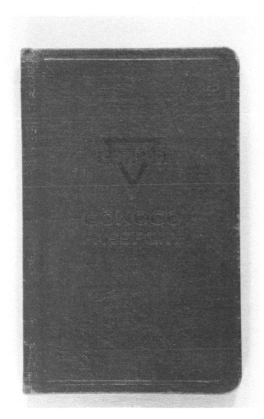

Your passport to Conoco, 2⅞″ x 4½″, 1931.

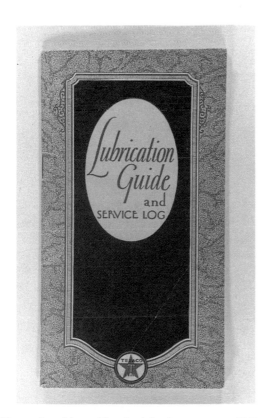

Texaco's guide and log for lube-ing your car, 3½″ x 6¼″.

The front of a thumb-flip movie book depicting a tire blowout crash, 2½″ x 2½″ from General Tire in the early 1920s.

Flipping the reverse side of General Tire's movie book shows the same crash in slow motion.

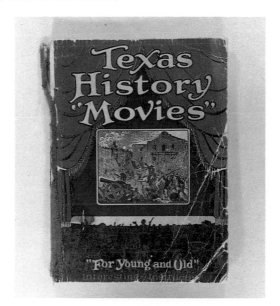

A Mobil Texas history booklet, "For Young and Old," 5¼″ x 7¼″.

SALT AND PEPPER SHAKERS

Mobilgas pump salt and pepper shakers.

Another set from Mobil.

Two battered Esso pump shakers.

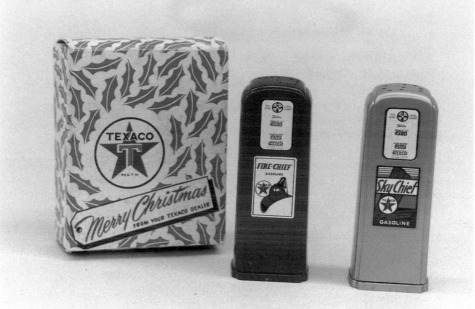

Fire Chief and Sky Chief gasoline pump shakers from Texaco, with their Christmas-time gift box.

Esso shaker pumps, with their original box.

A pair of "crowned" pump shakers for Standard's Gold Crown and Red Crown gas

Red and yellow Shell shakers.

Shaker pumps for Milemaster and Super 5-D gas.

Bay's twin shaker gas pumps.

Rob-lon and Pure gas pump shakers.

Two gas pump shakers from Phillips 66.

Standard pump salt and pepper for White Crown and Red Crown gasoline, without the "crown" top ornaments.

Gulf pump salt and pepper for "Crest" and "No Nox" gasoline

D-X shakers.

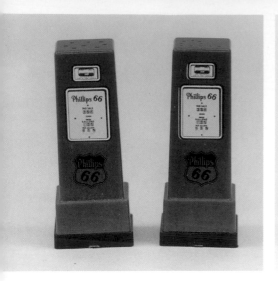

More Phillips 66 gas pump shakers.

A pair of Humble gas pump salt and peppers.

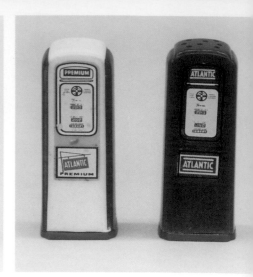

A red, white and blue set of Atlantic gas shakers.

Conoco and Super Conoco gasoline pump salt and pepper.

Esso shaker pumps.

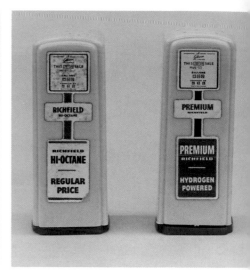

Gas pump shakers for Richmond Premium and Hi-Octane.

Salt and Pepper from Flying A Stations.

A plastic shaker pump from Baker's Service, a Phillips 66 station.

Amoco and American gas pump shakers.

CERAMICS

A dinner plate from the Frank Kent Ford dealership...

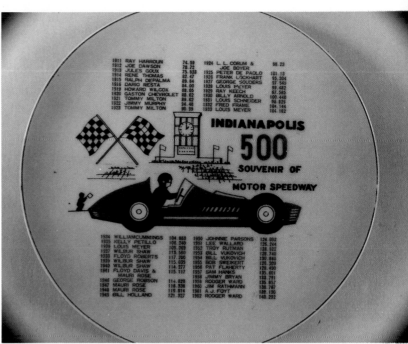

A souvenir plate from the Indy 500, 1963.

...with the matching cup (3⅞″ x 2¼″) and saucer (6″ diam.).

A Texaco mug, with its logo on the telltale "marine" flag.

A Buick cup, 3¾″ x 2⅜″, and saucer, 6⅛″ diam.

A second Texaco marine mug, 3¼″ x 2⅛″

A Ford Rotunda dinner plate, 6⅛″ diam.

A segmented dinner plate from Ford, 10⅜″ diam.

A Ford oval serving plate, 4⅛″ x 5½″.

Dinner and salad plates (7⅛″ and 5¾″ diameters, respectively) with the Mobil marine flag logo.

The matching mug, 37/16″ x 3½″ tall, from Mobil marine.

A Ford china coffee mug, 3⅜″ x 3″ tall.

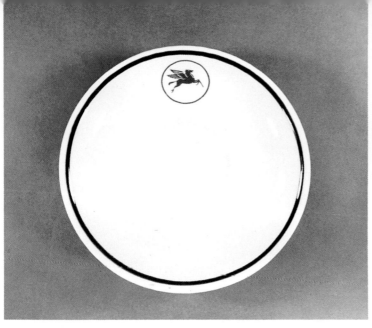

A salad plate from Mobil, 7″ diam., featuring the flying horse logo.

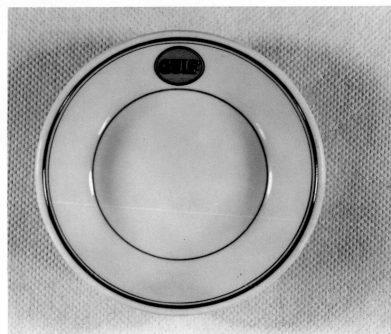

Gulf's butter dish, 5″ diam.

A salad plate, 7″ diam., and a dessert plate, 4¾″, from Mobil.

A 9″ dinner plate from Phillips 66.

The Esso marine flag on 3½″ tall salt and pepper shakers.

A cup, 3″ x 2¾″, and saucer, 5⅞″ diam., from Esso's marine division.

DESK ACCESSORIES

A 1950s brass pen holder from Mobil, 3″ x 4″

A brass paperweight from Mobil.

Paper clips from Texaco, Paragon Oil and Phillips 66.

From the 1950s, a brass Mobil bookend, 5¼″ x 4¾″.

A painted sea shell paperweight from Ft. Worth, Texas in the 1970s.

A Chevrolet paperweight from the 1930s, 4½″ long.

Lion Petroleum's mascot is about to start the hunt, on this bronze-look paperweight, 3½″ long.

A clipboard clip from an Iowa tire dealer.

A brass clipboard from Sell in the 1930s, 4″ x 8⅜″.

Texaco blotters circa 1918, one Atlantic blotter from the 1940s.

A desk top box in the shape of a Firestone battery, 2⅜″ x 3½″ x 2⅞″ tall.

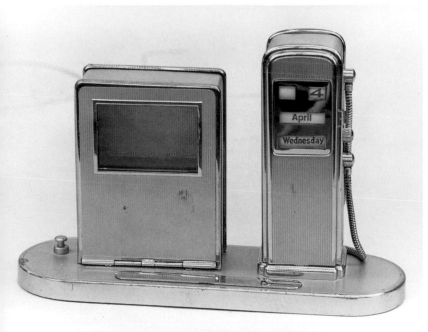

A combination desk calendar/cigarette case, 4¾ x 7″.

A Ford clipboard clip, circa 1918.

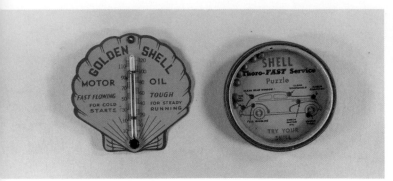

A metal thermometer from Shell, 2½″ x 2½″.

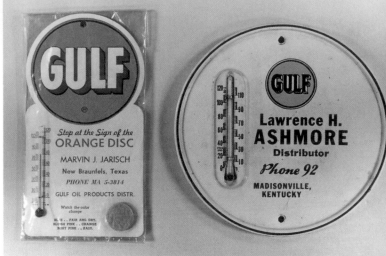

Thermometers from Gulf—one in paper, 3¼″ x 6¼″, and one in metal, 6″ diam.

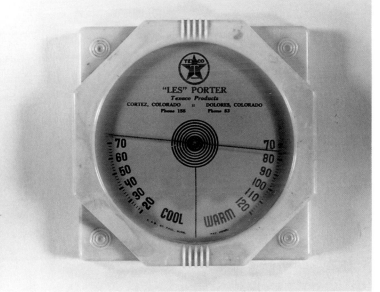

A plastic Texaco thermometer, 5¾″ x 5¾″.

Thermometers from Pure (plastic, 2⅛″ x 7″), Texaco (metal, 2½″ x 6¼″) and Champlin (plastic, 2¼″ x 7″).

A Willard Batteries thermometer from the 1960s, 11¾″ diam.

This Nash thermometer promises it will "go up in '56," 2½″ x 4¼″.

TIMEPIECES

Marine Oils/ Vacuum Oil Co. classically shaped miniature shelf clock, 2¼″ x 2½″.

A Seiberling "will be back" clock of lithographed tin, 7¾″ x 10″.

Fisk's "Time to Re-Tire" clock fits inside a rubber model tire, 7″ in diameter.

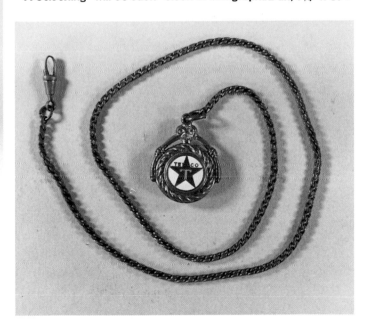

An early Texaco pocket fob and chain.

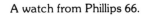

A watch from Phillips 66.

GAMES AND PUZZLES

Kids could play at being mechanics, troubleshooting on long car rides with Shell's 2⅜" hand-held game.

An 11½" x 14¾" puzzle from Texaco, autographed by Ed Wynn, "The Perfect Fool."

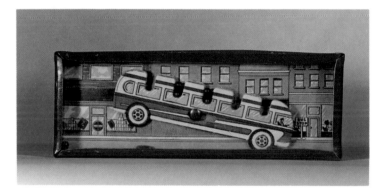

Another early hand-held game, 2½" x 7", with a precariously tilting omnibus.

A 9¾" x 13¼" puzzle from 1933: pretty little girls on a pleasure cruise refuel their boat with Pan-Am gasoline.

A very early palm game from Germany, 2⅛".

POP GUNS

American Gas's paper pop gun, 8″ long, asks customers to submit slogan ideas for $1000 of cash prizes.

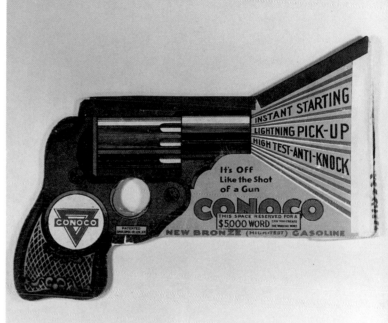

Conoco's 8″ paper pop gun brags that your car will be "Off Like the Shot of a Gun" with their high-test, anti-knock gasoline.

Sinclair's "Bang Gun" promises lots of fun for kids lucky enough to collect this 8″ keepsake.

TOY GASOLINE TRUCKS

This Gulf tanker is a Walt Reach Toy by Courtland, 12½".

A streamlined "Buddy L" Shell truck, 17½" long.

A Mobil tanker from Marusan of Japan, 16" long.

An Arcade Mack oil tank truck, 7".

A Mobil gas tanker, complete with tool box, from Japan, 11" long.

Marx's Cities Service tanker, 18½".

A Sinclair gas tanker by Marx, 18½" long.

Another Mobil tanker from Japan, this one 11½" long.

A lithographed tin "Junior" oil tank truck by Chein, 8½" long.

From Japan, a friction-motor powered Esso tank truck, 9½" long, and its box.

A mechanical gas tanker by Louis Marx, 14½" long, and its original packaging.

TOY SERVICE STATIONS AND GARAGES

A "Lubritorium" car wash, 6″x 9″, from Marx

"For the young car owner"—*very* young, that is. This Wannatoy station is made of paper. Many of the popular toys of the 1920s through the present time have been replicas of gas stations. With each reflecting their particular era, they have become very desirable and collectible.

A Mobil station, 4½″ x 8⅛″ of lithographed tin, made in Japan circa 1959.

A "Cragston" Mobilgas station, 6″ x 9¾″ of lithographed tin from the late 1950s.

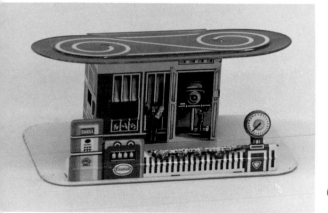

A miniature service station made in Germany in the '50s, 3″ x 5″ of lithographed tin.

"Line-Mar" Cities Service station, 6″ x 10½″ of lithographed tin, made in Japan in the 1950s.

A "Jane Francis" brand Gulf station from the 1940s, folded paper with metal trucks, 11¼″ x 15″.

A detailed model garage; the doors swing open for two 1920s-style cars. Made by Tipp, Germany.

A lithographed tin miniature fill-up station, with car, from occupied Japan. 1⅞″ x 2¾″, 1949.

A wooden garage model from Chevrolet, made in the early 1930s, 19" x 23".

The cardboard "Busy Airport Garage" stands 10½" wide x 10" tall. Made by Marx.

A Marx lithographed tin service station, earmarked for the youngest of municipal airport customers. 5⅜" x 6½", circa 1934.

A local service station complete with a car to scale by Marx, 5⅜" x 6½", lithographed tin, circa 1934.

A "Wyandotte" Shell station, tin with a "brick" look. 11½" x 15¾", circa 1937.

A German service station made of lithographed tin in the 1950s, 2⅝" x 3⅞".

This "Built Rite" Shell station in cardboard is from the 1930s. 13½"
x 17½", including the driveway.

A "Built Rite" cardboard garage and showroom, 10" x 14½", from
the late 1930s.

"Built Rite's" elaborate boxed toy parking garage,
filling station and Chrysler service station, circa
1939. Cardboard, 14" x 20½".

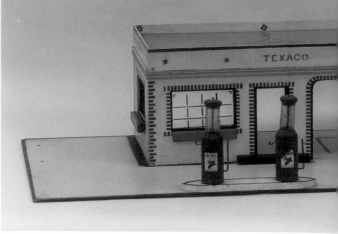

Another "Rich" Texaco station of wood, 18¼" x 27½".

A Schuco service station model from West Germany in the 1950s, 3½" x 6".

Germany's Lehmann Toys made this "petrol station and racing car garage" in 1934, with the Shell logo, three cars and two airflows. Station, 4" x 5⅜" x 3½". Garage, 3½" x 4½". Cars, 3⅞".

A German-made Schuco way station (3½" x 7¾") with a gasoline truck (4¼"), featuring a map of the Netherlands, Denmark and northern Germany.

Bottom left:
A "Rich" wooden Texaco station, 12½" x 14".

Bottom right:
A fancy wooded station with plastic accessories, 17" x 23" from Ideal.

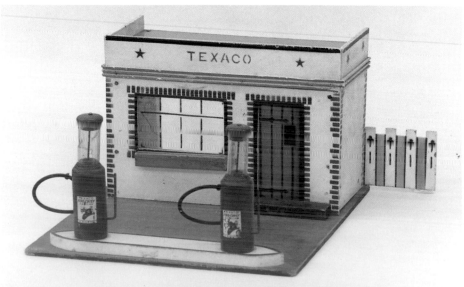

A lithographed tin station with car from Distler, in Germany. 2¾″ x 4″.

"Day and Night Service," promises the sign between two pumps, at this Bluebird station, 6½″ x 12″. Gasoline delivery truck, 7″.

The Tower Garage, a large "Rich" station at 12″ x 27″.

This station, 7½″ x 11¾″, is lithographed tin from Superior.

The Arcade station, wooden with cast iron gas pumps and a metal grease rack, 12½″ x 12½″.

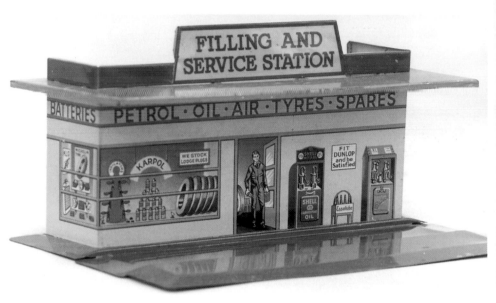

From England, a "Dinky" station of lithographed tin, 5¼″ x 7⅝″ from the 1950s.

An 11″ x 17″ Gull station, complete with car wash, air pump and grease rack. Made by Marx.

A cheerfully painted wooden station (10″ x 12″) from Arcade, complete with cast iron pumps. Shown with a tow-truck and a car.

Hullco Toy's model "Toygas" filling station, 12″ x 13″. Box pictured on page 150 upper left.

A Keystone Garage model, 7⅜″ x 9⅞″, with box.

A lithographed tin garage box by Chein, 3⅞″ x 6⅞″.

Londontoy's "build your own" service station, in a 7½″ x 13¼″ box.

A service station you can hide in your hand, 1⅝″ x 2⅝″ of lithographed tin.

Schoenhut's Hollywood Builder set makes "one gas station," from a 8¼″ x 8¼″ box. No. 5.

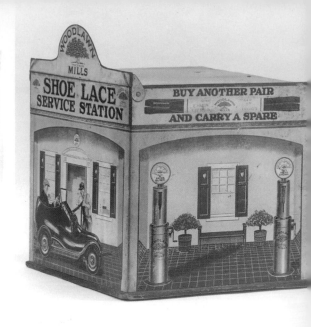

Packaging for the Toygas filling station.

This Woodlawn Mills Shoe Lace Service Station, whimsically illustrated on the front...

Wyandotte's Garage tin with gas pumps, 8½″ square.

Milton Bradley's wooden self-assembly "Bumpalow" garage, 6″ x 10½″ if you put it together right.

...hides drawers full of shoelaces in the back. 11″ x 11¼″.

This unique station model, 8¾″ x 10½″, is made of Lincoln Logs, ceramic brick, paper and wood.

A 9″ x 15″ tin by Gibbs has been illustrated in great detail with layered roof tiles, fancy brick-work, a pitcher on the curb, and even a window box full of flowers.

The grease rack of a Shell station, from a German manufacturer. 1⅞″ x 3⅞″.

Two versions of a Japanese-made gas station model for Mobil, 1¾″ x 2⅝″.

Another Gibbs model, of lithographed tin is 8⅜″ x 11⅝″ with a fold-up driveway.

A miniature from pre-war Japan, 1 15/16″ x 2⅞″.

A German Arnold station, with clear windows into the occupied office. 6¾″ x 13½″.

A Wyandotte piece, 3⅞″ x 5″ in lithographed tin.

Marx's brightly-painted gas pump island, 2⅝″ x 9½″ with old-style glass globes atop each pump.

This service station model, "Tunnel Service Incorporated," is one 7½″ long section of a road set by Marx.

One of Fairylite's "foreign" garage models, with gas pumps and two cars. 3½″ x 4″.

A hand-painted ceramic filling station, 2¼″ x 4″.

A coordinating pair of gas pump islands by Marx, 2⅝″ x 9½″, again with old-fashioned globes.

A "Roadside Rest" service station, by Marx. Gasoline pumps, an air pump, motor oil, a grease rack and an outdoor lunch counter fit into the 13⅝″ x 10⅛″ model from 1934.

Marx's modern version of the Roadside Rest filling station, with its box.

A few miles down the road...Marx's "Sunny Side Service Station." Very similar to the Roadside model, this features an indoor luncheonette.

A more modern version of Marx's lithographed tin rest stop, with a fancy roadster and updated electric gasoline and air pumps. Circa 1940, 13⅝" x 10⅛".

A steel Texaco station with plastic accessories and its original box, 15" x 24½".

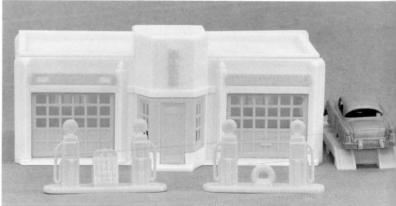

A filling station with a double-doored "lubritorium," or *carwash*, and a car on risers off to the side.

A lithographed tin Shell station, 15" x 24½".

A Lithographed tin service station from "Superior," 14″ x 25″.

A "Rich" wood station, 10″ x 18½″, featuring a grease pit, a repair center and a show room.

A boxed "Mini Service Station," 13½″ x 17″.

A cardboard "garage," 2½″ x 4¾″, from Rockwood & Company; the contents of the station were made of milk chocolate.

A "Buddy L" tin Texaco station, 18″ x 24″, circa 1957.

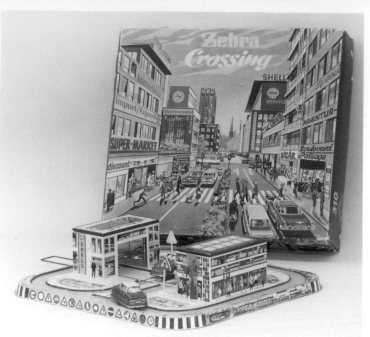

A wind-up model from Technofix of Germany, 12" x 13".

A wind-up, rotating driving scenario from D.R.G.M. in Germany, with a gas station at the hub. 8⅜" x 8¾", of lithographed tin.

A complete "Blue Box" service station, with Shell accessories. 14¼" x 12".

"My Merry" paper Gulf station from 1969, 6½" x 8".

A Firestone station from 1949, 15¾" x 24" of lithographed tin.

MINIATURE GAS PUMPS

"Chein" lithographed tin gas pump cart, 8" tall from the 1920s. Texaco Filling Station.

Right: "Mohawk" Playgas miniature pump, lithographed tin with a glass cylinder, 7¾" tall, circa 1930; left: "Mohawk" Playgas pump model, lithographed tin, missing a glass cylinder. 10⅝" tall, circa 1930.

This cardboard Texaco pump from 1939, 32½" tall, featured Fire Chief gasoline.

Circa 1920 from Germany, Doll Toy Co.'s gas station is 7½" x 11¾" x 9¾" tall, and features miniature glass bottles and canisters.

Another Doll Toy Co. model station, 4¾" x 9" x 7¾", circa 1920 and featuring rubber tubing, a glass "light bulb" and glass bottles.

This gas pump is actually a 1925 candy container, 4⅛″ tall.

Texaco's pencil case, shaped like a Fire Chief gasoline pump.

Left: Germany's Doll Toy Co. made this 3¾″ x 5¼″ oil dispenser model in 1920; right: a portable oil cart model from Germany, by the Doll Toy Co. in 1920. 3¼″ x 5″.

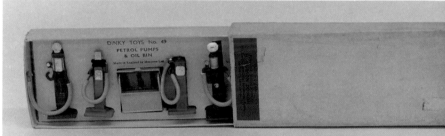

From England, a set of "Dinky"'s miniature gas pumps, from 1½″ to 2¼″ tall.

Wardie Toys manufactured these cast-metal pumps featuring many brands of gasoline, all approximately 3″ high

Left: A pressed metal gas pump with a glass cylinder and rope trim, 9″; right: A pressed tin gas pump from the U.S. Gasoline Company by Hullco Toys, 10″ tall.

Playgas' model pump and a waiting car.

From the Novelet Toy Company in the 1920s, this miniature gas pump stands 13¼″ tall.

By Schuco in Germany, an ICA pump standing 3¾″ tall, and a wooden Shell oil pump standing 3½″ tall.

Kilgore Manufacturing Company's cast iron gas pump model, from the 1920s, with box.

Gong Bell Manufacturers made this toy gasoline pump, 17⅞″ tall, in the mid-1920s.

Arcade gas pumps, 6″ tall.

Brightly colored gas pumps, 6″ high, possibly by Marx.

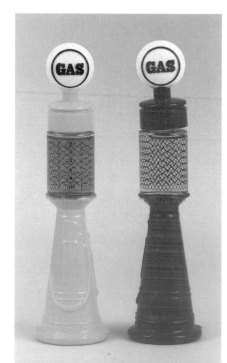

Gas pump-shaped bottles from Avon from the 1970s, 9⅜″ tall.

Glass candy container in the shape of a gasoline pump, 4⅛″ tall, circa 1935

A bilingual Shell pump from Germany, 7″ tall, in plastic.

J. H. Millstein Candy Co. produced these gas pump candy dispensers, 6⅛″ tall.

BANKS

An Arcade Toys gas pump bank, in cast iron, 5¾" tall, shown with two Arcade Toys cast iron gas pumps, 4⅜". Some of the popular giveaways were the banks that represented and advertised the different oil company products.

Esso's mascot, in bright red plastic, salutes those who save their pennies.

Mobil Oil's gray piggy-bank pledges that their Federal Credit Union is "Not for profit, not for charity, but for service."

Left: "Save a Barrel of Money," urges Cross Country Products; right: West Chemical Products's orange and black change bank, with a list of locations circling the base and the advice "Save Best with West" stenciled on top.

A pair of green "Fat Man" banks from Texaco and from Conoco.

Are your pennies safer in a bank disguised as a can of motor oil? These are from Havoline, Panolene and Triton.

161

Banks resembling motor oil cans from Whiz Motor Rythm (sic), Miracle Power and En-Ar-Co.

A Dodge Dart bank, and a Mobil Lubricant bank.

Wolf's Head, Shell and Super-Shell motor oil, advertised on penny banks.

Two motor oil can banks from Pennzoil.

A coin bank from Pennzoil advertising motor oil, and another from Havoline advertising their "supreme" motor oil.

Mobiloil's flying horse decorates this bank.

Can banks from Cities Service...

Left to right: Mobil's bright red "piggy" bank, stamped with the flying horse logo; a gleaming gold-colored piggy bank, with embossed letters reading "Save with Marathon"; a bronze-like finish for this dinosaur bank from Sinclair.

A change bank from Zephyr.

...from Diamond and from Texaco.

Banks shaped like miniature gas pumps, from (left to right) Pure Premium, Atlantic and Billups Premium.

Sunoco's Dynalube, Royal Triton and Union Long Distance Purple cans converted to change banks.

You can count your change through this transparent, 5½" wide bank from Sohio.

Motor oil and anti-freeze from Pennzoil, Sinclair and Thermo-Royal, used as banks.

Left: Chevrolet's map of the world appears on this globe-shaped bank; right: "Save Your Pennies" in Buick's Fireball Eight bank.

Marathon, Crown and Veedol's bank cans.

The back of the red Buick ball bank exclaims that the Fireball is the "Best Buick Yet!"

"See What You Save," says Mobilgas's transparent bank.

A square-shaped glass bank from Standard.

Esso's see-through coin bank.

Drydene and Allis-Chalmers can banks.

A Mobile can masquerades as a coin bank.

Plastic banks from Shell and from Sinclair.

Conoco, Cities Service and Gulf can banks.

Bank cans from Tower Oil Co., Standard and Cities Service.

Royal Triton and Veedol can banks.

Oil-can shaped metal banks from Arco and RPM, and a battery-shaped bank from Atlas.

Esso's clear red plastic fire truck bank.

This gas pump-shaped coin bank from Texaco stands 9″ tall.

Gull Petroleum's banks, one painted copper and the other red and black. New, not old.

Wolf's Head, Triton and Diamond can banks.

Dodge's barrels (one made to look like old-fashioned wood, the other modern metal) are actually change banks.

Sohio and Iso-Vis motor oil can banks.

Can banks from Illini, Mobiloil and Amoco.

Bardahl, Pennzoil and Allstate's can banks.

Painted metal gas-pump banks from Power-X, Sinclair and Sunoco.

A 4" plastic bank from Gulf advertises solar heat.

Can banks from Conoco, Cen-Pe-Co and RPM.

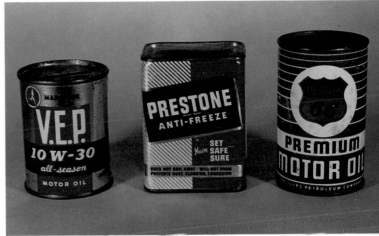

V.E.P., Prestone and Phillips 66 can banks.

Tagolene, Amalie and Farm-Oyl banks.

Amoco, Veedol and Johnson motor oil cans double as banks.

A very decorative can bank from Thermo anti-freeze, and motor-oil cans from Purelube and Structo.

Sohio and Phillips 66 square banks in glass.

Esso's square glass bank.

A trio of can banks representing different Phillips 66 products.

A fold-up cardboard bank for keeping the "up to 2 cents a gallon" drivers could save with Sunoco's Dynafuel.

Can banks from Allstate, En-Ar-Co and Schaeffer's.

Can banks from Fram, Colgra and Wolf's Head.

Two plastic banks.

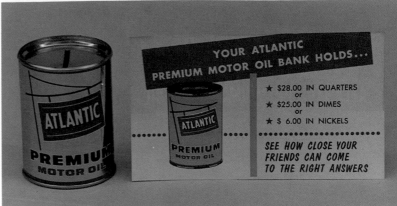

A change bank from Atlantic, with its educational packaging.

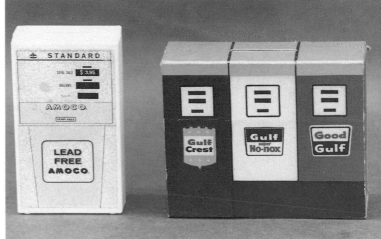

Shaped like gas pumps, banks from Amoco and from Gulf.

Mobilgas and Mobilgas Special banks in the shape of gas pumps.

Atlantic and Dodge can banks.

Sohio, Cities Service and Castrol can banks.

A "Sav-A-Vacation" bank from the Shell Touring Service, and a gas pump shaped bank from Sinclair Power-X.

Oil can bank from Mobil.

Can banks from Oilzum and Drydene.

Two baseball banks.

OTHER TOYS

Sinclair's paper replica for kids of an attendant's cap.

A toy auto jack from Simplex, 3″ high from 1925.

A mechanical "Giant Tire Toy" from U.S. Royal, 10″ tall.

"Buddy Lee Phillips" doll from Phillips 66, 13″ tall.

Douglas Oil Company's "Freddy Fast" doll, 7½″ tall.

The "Danny O'Day" puppet from Texaco, 24″ tall.

A plastic firefighter's helmet from Texaco, 8″ x 14″, circa 1950.

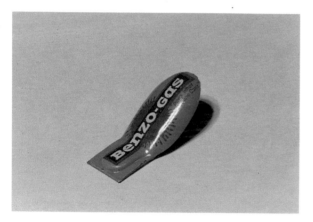

A "clicker" toy from Benzo Gas, 1¾″.

Texaco's promotional oil tank ship, 27″ long.

A spinning top from Gulf, 1½″.

"DinoSoap" in the shape of an oil truck from Sinclair, 4″ long.

"DinoSoap" in the shape of a dinosaur, 5″ long.

172

PRICE GUIDE

To Gas Station Collectibles

Values vary immensely according to the condition of the piece, the location of the market, and the overall quality of the design and manufacturer. While one must make their own decisions, we can offer a guide. These are estimates of retail prices of pieces in excellent condition.

The lefthand number is the page. The letters following the page denote the position of the photo on the page: T=top; L=left; TL=top left; TR=top right; C=center; CL=center left; CR=center right; R=right; B=bottom;BL=bottom left; BR=bottom right. In photos with more than one object, they are identified. The right hand numbers are the estimated retail price ranges inU.S. dollars.

4	TL	800
	TR	500-600
	BL	1200-1500
	BR	2800-3000
5	TL	600-800
	TR	250-300
	CL	800-1000
	CR	700-800
	BL	1100-1400
	BR	1600-2000
6	TL	400-600
	TR	1200-1600
	CL	500-700
	CR	600-700
	BR	1200-1500
7	TL	400-800
	TR	300-400
	CR	900-1200
	BL	350
	BR	350-450
8	TL	900-1200
	TR	200-250
	CL	350-450
	CR	1800-2300
	BL	250-350
	BR	300-400
9	TL	350-450
	TR	600-1400
	CL	200-900
	CR	600-800
	BL	1800-2200
	BR	800-1100
10	TL	900-1200

	TR	250-350
	CL	500-600
	CR	300-400
	BL	400-550
	BR	250-350
11	TL	250-350
	TR	500-700
	CL	200-300
	CR	250-300
	BL	800-1100
	BR	600-800
12	TL	650-750
	TR	1400-1600
	CL	500-600
	CR	3000-3500
	BL	1800-2200
	BR	300-500
13	TL	500-700
	TR	1000-1200
	CL	500-700
	CR	1200-1400
	B	600-800
14	TL	900-1200
	TR	250-300
	CL	250-350
	CR	1400-1700
	BL	400-600
	BR	250-300
15	TL	700-800
	TR	175-250
	CL	300-400
	CR	150-250
	BL	400-500

	BR	200-300
16	TL	150-250
	TR	150-250
	CL	600-800
	CR	125-200
	BL	150-250
	BR	600-800
17	TL	200-300
	TR	150-250
	CL	400-500
	CR	250-350
	BL	300-400
	BR	1800-2200
18	TL	400-600
	TR	300-400
	CL	600-800
	CR	200-250
	BL	400-600
	BR	500-600
19	TL	250-350
	TR	200-225
	CL	300-500
	BL	250-300
	BR	200-225
20	TL	150-225
	TR	300-400
	CL	150-200
	CR	300-450
	BL	150-200
	BR	175-225
21	TL	600-800
	TR	200-300
	CL	300-400
	CR	400-600
	BL	150-200
	BR	400-600
22	TL	200-250
	TR	150-200
	BL	400-600
	BR	300-400
23	TL	150-200
	TR	250-300
	BL	150-200
	BR	250-350
24	TL	90-110
	CL	70-95
	CR	25-30
	BL	110-120
	BR	90-115
25	TL	25-30
	TR	35-55
	BL	25-30
	BR	30-45
26	TL	8-12
	TR	5-10

	BL	8-12
	BR	5-10
27	TL	10-12
	TR	12-15
	BL	10-12
	BR	10-12
28	TL	5-10
	TR	5-10
	BL	5-10
	BR	5-10
29	TL	5-10
	TR	5-10
	BL	5-10
	BR	5-10
30	TL	5-8
	TR	75-110
	CR	75-80
	BL	10-22
	BR	600-750
31	TL	45-55
	TR	45-55
	CL	40-55
	CR	40-50
	B	18-25
32	TL	25-30
	TR	35-45
	CL	30-35
	CR	15-25
	BL	10-15
	BR	15-25
33	TL	10-15
	TR	10-18
	CL	15-25
	CR	10-15
	CL	25-30
	CR	10-15
34	TL	15-22
	TR	25-35
	CL	15-20
	CR	20-30
	BL	15-22
	BR	10-15
35	TL	18-25
	TR	10-18
	CL	15-18
	CR	75-80
	BL	18-25
36	TL	15-20
	TR	20-25
	CL	18-25
	CR	20-30
	BR	25-35
37	TL	18-20
	TR	10-15
	CL	15-20

No.	Pos	Value		No.	Pos	Value		No.	Pos	Value		No.	Pos	Value
	CR	10-15			BL	18-22			BR	24-30, left			TR	45-55
	BL	25-35			BR	30-35				20-25, right			CL	20-25
	BR	10-15		48	TL	20-25				22-30, bottom			CR	40-50
38	TL	25-35			TR	25-35		59	TL	50-60, left			BR	10
	TR	40-70			CL	15-22				125-140, right		71	TL	25-30
	CL	25-35			BL	15-25			TR	120-145			TC	22-25
	CR	10-20			BR	65-70			CL	30-45			TR	22-25
	BL	18-25		49	TL	60-80			CR	12-15			BL	22-28
39	TL	10-20			TR	30-40			BL	15-25 ea.			BR	40-50
	TR	25-35			CL	25-30			BR	15-35 ea.		72	TL	10-15
	CL	10-18			BL	18-25		60	TL	40-50			TR	35-50
	CR	25-35			BR	25-30			TR	25-35			BL	18-22
	BL	10-15		50	TL	45-70			BL	25-35			BR	35-50
40	TL	20-25			TR	40-65			BR	40-45		73	TL	40
	TR	15-25			CL	18-20		61	TL	40-45			TR	25-35
	CL	18-25			BL	20-45			CL	25-30			BL	25-45
	CR	18-22			BR	20-40			CR	45-50			BR	25
	BL	10-15		51	TL	30-35			BL	30-40		74	TL	45-75
	BR	18-20			CL	25-30		62	TL	20-30			TR	45-65
41	TL	18-22			CR	15-20			TR	18-25			CL	35-40
	TR	20-30			BL	35-55			CL	25-35			BL	35-45
	CL	20-30		52	TL	35-75			CR	12-20			BR	10-20
	CR	10-18			TR	40-90			BR	22-25		75	TL	18-25
	BL	18-28			CL	110-140		63	TL	30-40			TR	20-35
	BR	18-25			CR	35-60			CR	25-30			CL	25-35
42	TL	15-20			BL	110-150			BL	25-30			CR	25-35
	TR	18-25		53	TL	15-20		64	T	18-25			BL	18-22
	CL	10-15			TR	25-30			C	25-35		76	T	25-30
	CR	18-25			CL	10-15			B	18-25			C	12-18 ea.
	BL	18-25			CR	20-30		65	TL	22-38			B	75-110
	BR	18-25			BL	10-15			TR	22-25		77	TL	16-22
43	TL	18-25			BR	20-25			C	25-30			TR	10-15
	TR	25-30		54		25-45 ea.			B	35-45			BL	125-145
	CL	18-25		55	TR	125-145		66	TL	22-25			BR	12-18
	CR	25-35				25-45 ea.			TR	22-25		78	TL	22-25
	B	20-30		56	TL	25 ea.			CL	10-15			CL	18-30
44	TL	20-30			TR	150-175			CR	10-15			CR	40
	TR	10-18			CL	18-35, small			BR	28-35			BR	10-18 ea.
	CL	10-15				30-45, large		67	TL	30-35		79	TL	175-225
	CR	18-25			CR	45-55			TR	25-30			TR	325-450
	BL	10-15			BL	25			CL	35-45			BL	110-155
	BR	10-18			BR	25-35			CR	10-15			BR	75-110
45	TL	18-20		57	TL	25-45 ea.			BL	110-135		80	TL	65-75
	TR	10-18			TR	85-90		68	TL	18-20			TR	110-140
	CL	10-18			CL	90-110, top			TC	35-45			CL	90-110
	BR	18-22				95-115, bot.			TR	45-50			B	65-255
	BL	15-25			CR	90-110			BL	25-40		81	TL	130-200
46	TL	10-18			CR	125-130			BC	45-60			TR	85-110
	TR	25-35			BL	123-145			BR	45-60			BL	40, left
	C	15-25			BR	70-90		69	TL	50-55				55, right
	B	15-20		58	TL	40-45			TR	18-30			BR	110-140
47	TL	10-15			TR	30-40 ea.			CL	50-55		82	TL	25-30
	TR	18-20			CL	35-40			BL	28-35			TC	70-85
	CL	30-35			CR	25-30			BR	18-20			TR	70-85
	CR	25-35			BL	65-80		70	TL	30-50			CL	65-80

C 70-85
CR 70-85
BL 55-70
BR 90-100
83 TL 70-85
TR 45-55
CL 70-85
C 700-850
CR 40-55
BL 95-120
BR 190-210
84 TL 35-40
TR 45-65
CR 95-125
BL 25-35
BR 30-45
85 TL 35-40, left
30-40, right
TR 35-40
C 90-95
BR 350-425
BL 80-110
86 TL 70-85
TC 65-75
TR 150-200
BR 65-75, left
70-80, right
87 TL 75-90, left
45-65, right
TR 600-800
BL 25-30
88 TR 65-125
CR 18-20 ea.
BL 90-120 ea.
BR 18-20 ea.
89 TR 30-45
CL 5-12 ea.
CR 5-12 ea.
BL 5-12 ea.
90 TL 22-25 ea.
CR 35-50 ea.
BL 500
BR 1-2
91 TL 25-30
TR 25-30
CL 25-35
CR 10-15
BL 25-45
92 TL 90-125
TR 15-22
CL 25-30
CR 10-15
BL 8-10
93 TL 40-45, left
45-50, right

TR 18-25
CL 12-15
CR 18-25
BL 12-15, left
12-18, right
BR 12-15
B 20-35
94 TL 25-30 ea.
TR 18-20 ea.
CL 10-14
CR 15-18 ea.
BL 15-18 ea.
BR 8-12
B 10-14
95 TL 25-35, left
TR 90-110
CL 22-25, left
20-25, right
CR 40, top
110-125, btm.
BL 10-12 ea.
96 TL 18-25, ea.
TR 22-28, left
15-22, right
CL 22-25, left
18-25, right
CR 140-185, left
110-125, right
BL 10-12, ea.
97 TL 25-35
TR 40-50
CL 25
CR 90-125, left
80-100, right
BL 18-22 ea.
98 TL 25-45 ea.
99-103 18-70 ea.
104-106 40-70 ea.
107-109 25-55 ea.
110 TR 135-170
BL 125-150
111 TL 25-30 ea.
TR 30-40 ea.
CL 20-45 ea.
CR 15-20
BL 20-30
112 TL 60-80 ea.
TR 20-30 ea.
C 20-22, far left
15-20, left
15-20, right
17-20, far rt.
BL 20-30
BR 5
113 40-70 ea.

114 TL 10-15
TR 30-40, top
40-45, bottom
CL 18-25
C 65-90
CR 60-80
BL 10-20 ea.
BR 10-15
115 TL 15-25 ea.
TR 18-25
CL 15-20, left
12-18, right
CR 18-20
BL 15-30
BR 15-25
BL 10-22
116 TL 8-10 ea.
TR 130-155
CL 8-10 set
BL 10-15
BR 8-20
117 TL 22-30
TR 40-60
CL 40-60
CR 25-30
118 TL 10-15
TC 110-150
TR 25
CL 15-20
CR 40-50
BL 20-25
BR 25-45 ea.
119 TL 65-90
TR 25-35 ea.
CL 20-35
CR 20-35 ea.
120 TL 18-25
TR 45-75
CL 175-225
CR 10-20
BL 15-22
121 TL 30-40
TR 30-40
CL 60-90
CR 15-25
BL 35-45 ea.
122 TL 290-320
TR 900-1400
BL 800-1250
BR 550-670
123 TL 650-875
C 650-875
TR 900-1250
BL 1000-1400
BR 450-550

124 TL 10-25
TR 10-25
BL 18-25
BR 25-35
125 TL 30-45
C 30-45
TR 25-35
CL 18-22
BR 18-22
126 TL 25-30
TR 22-25
BL 18-25
BR 18-22
127 TL 25-30
TR 10-15
CR 10-15
BL 25-40
BR 10-18
128 TL 50-60
TR 40-50
CL 75-80
BR 45-55
BL 25-30
129 TL 125-135
TC 90-100
TR 80-90
CL 60-70
C 50-60
CR 25-30
BL 60-70
BC 65-75
BR 85-95
130 TL 25-30
TC 25-30
TR 45-50
CL 65-75
C 25-30
CR 70-80
BL 90-125
BC 10-15
BR 90-100
131 TL 15-18
TR 30-45
CL 18-25
CR 30-45
BL 40-45
BR 40-50
132 TL 445-60
TR 45-65
CL 20-30
CL 50-60
BL 30
BR 45
133 TL 35-45
TR 30-35

CL 25-30
CR 75-80
BL 35-45
BR 60-70
134 TL 125-135
TR 175-185
CL 95
CR 30-40
BL 12-18 ea.
BR 135-145
B 60-80
135 TL 10-12
TR 125-135
CL 20-40
CR 30
BL 75-85
BR 15-20
136 CR 20-25
137 TL 150 175
TR 90-110
CL 90-125
CR 175
BL 85-95
138 TL 25-50
CL 25-50
BL 80-110
BR 25-45
139 TL 20-35
CR 20-35
BL 20-35
140 TL 275-325
C 150-200
CL 175-275
CR 125-190
B 130-175
141 TR 300-350
CR 150-225
CL 140-180
BL 140-180
BR 85-175
B no price
142 TR 120-200
CR 45-75
BL 75-100
BR 75-150
143 TR 95-175
CL 175-225
BR 2200-2600
BL 75-125
144 TL 225 250
TR 25-50
CL 300-450
CR 175-250
BR 275-400
145 TL 175-200

TR 75-125
CR 175-200
BR 175-250
146 TL 70-90
TR 175-250
CR 150-275
CL 850-1100
BL 325-500
BR 125-175
147 TR 350-400
C 200-275
BL 125-175
BR 125-175
148 TL 300-350
CR 220-250
CL 225-350
BR 575-650
149 TL 175-250
TR 275-300
CL 125-175
BL 350-400
BR 45-70
150 TR 1500-2000
CR 80-110
BL 150-225
151 TR 150-175
CL 300-400
BR 75-100 ea.
152 TL 85-110
TR 325-375
CL 140-160
CR 80-110
153 TL 170-225
TR 25-50
CR 150-200, left
120-175, right
CL 175-250
BR 250-375
BL 250-320
155 BL 250-320
156 TR 350-425
CR 40-50
157 TL 50-75
TC 155-190, left
200-300, right
TR 275-300
BL 850-975
BR 850-950
158 TL 275 350
TR 200-275, left
450 525, right
CL 75-125
CR 150-190
BL 650 750, left
150-200, right

BR 175-250
159 TL 75-110
TR no price
CR 30-50 ea.
BL 800-950
BR 175-225
160 TL 90-135 ea.
TR 250-275
CL 145-180
CR 35
BL 5-10
BR 70-110
161 TL 175-190, left
150-175, cnter
225-275, right
TR 45
CL 35
CR 45 ea.
BL 150, left
125, right
BR 35, left
60, center
40, right
162 TL 45-75 ea.
TR 25-35 ea.
CL 30-45 ea.
CR 25-35 ea.
BL 20-35 ea.
BR 25-35
B 25-35 ea.
163 TL 40-60 ea.
TR 18-20
CL 45, left
40, center
60, right
CR 60 ea.
BL 65
BR 40-60 ea.
164 TL 20-25 ea.
TR 30-40 ea.
CL 25-35 ea.
CR 30-40 ea.
BL 22
BR 40-65
B 40-65
165 TL 15-20 ea.
TR 15-20
CL 35-60
CR 20-30 ea.
LL 18 24 ea.
LR 18 20 ea.
BL 22-26
BR 18-22
166 TL 175-200
CL 45-60 ea.

CR 40-50 ea.
LL 45-60 ea.
LR 35-45
BL 40-55
167 TL 30-45 ea.
TR 45
CL 25-30 ea.
CR 50-60, left
35, center
30, right
LL 60, left
25 , center
25, right
LR 35, left
75, center
125, right
BL 75-80, left
60-75, center
35, right
168 TL 70-80 ea.
TR 40-60
CL 18-20 ea.
CR 25-35
BL 40-60 ea.
BR 12-15 ea.
169 TL 30, left
75, right
TR 25-30
CL 80-90 ea.
CR 10-15 ea.
BR 25-30 ea.
BL 12-15 ea.
170 TL 30-45 ea.
TR 75
BL 30-60 ea.
BR 65 ea.
171 TL 45
TR 225
CL 20-25
BL 25
BR 25
172 TL 150-175
TR 125
CL 15
CR 150-200
LL 12
LR 20-25
B 20-25